Poetry as Persuasion

The Life of Poetry

POETS ON THEIR ART AND CRAFT

CARL DENNIS

❧

Poetry as Persuasion

❧

The University of Georgia Press
Athens and London

Published by the University of Georgia Press
Athens, Georgia 30602
© 2001 by Carl Dennis
All rights reserved
Designed by Sandra Strother Hudson
Set in Minion by G & S Typesetters, Inc.
Printed and bound by McNaughton & Gunn
The paper in this book meets the guidelines for
permanence and durability of the Committee on
Production Guidelines for Book Longevity of the
Council on Library Resources.

Printed in the United States of America

05   04   03   02   01   C   5   4   3   2   1
05   04   03   02   01   P   5   4   3   2   1

Library of Congress Cataloging-in-Publication Data

Dennis, Carl.
Poetry as persuasion / Carl Dennis.
p. cm.—(The life of poetry)
Includes bibliographical references and index.
ISBN 0-8203-2255-5 (alk. paper)—ISBN 0-8203-2248-2
(pbk. : alk. paper)
1. Poetry—History and criticism—Theory, etc.   2. Persuasion (Psychology)   I. Title.   II. Series.
PN1031 .D377 2001
809.1—dc21   00-044728

British Library Cataloging-in-Publication Data available

FOR ROBERT DALY AND HOWARD WOLF

Contents

Acknowledgments

SEVERAL of these chapters began as lectures to be delivered during the residencies of the writing program at Warren Wilson College, and I want to thank the faculty and students of that program for their encouragement. I also want to thank Donald Revell, who published early versions of four chapters in the *Denver Quarterly* (chapters 1, 2, 4, and 5), and Stephen Donadio, who published a version of chapter 6 in the *New England Quarterly*. For her invaluable help in proofreading the book I am grateful to Lucy Carson. For advice about making the argument of the book as a whole more clear and forceful I am greatly indebted to Michael Collier. And for individual criticism on early drafts of all the chapters I am thankful to three friends: Robert Daly, Alan Feldman, and Martin Pops.

Poetry as Persuasion

Introduction

IN HIS WELL-KNOWN MAPPING of approaches to literature, M. H. Abrams distinguishes four different emphases depending on whether the critic chooses to relate the work to the world, to the audience, to the artist, or to the formal demands of the work itself. Thus the world, he points out, is central to criticism informed by Aristotle's notion of *mimesis,* which presents the work as the representation of a probable action; the audience is central in approaches like those of Horace or Pope, which present the poem as a means to delight and instruct the reader; the artist is central in Wordsworth's aesthetic, which regards the poem as the expression of the poet's feelings; and the poem is treated in isolation in any criticism that emphasizes the relation among its formal elements.[1] Most critical stances incorporate at least some of the others in subordinate ways. So Aristotle argues that the imitation of a tragic action will produce the emotions of pity and fear in the audience; and he treats the work formally in stipulating that to possess beauty it must be an organic whole to which nothing can be added or removed without diminishing its coherence. But though most critical stances are mixed, most critics choose one to define what they consider central in judging a work, and my approach in this book is no exception. I choose here to focus on relating the poem to its audience, offering an example of what Abrams calls "pragmatic criticism," which treats the poem as an instrument for producing certain attitudes in the reader. And as is the case with most rhetorically based criticism, my emphasis is practical. Though I hope this book proves useful to any reader interested in poetic rhetoric, I am writing in particular for practicing poets, especially for those new enough to their craft to be helped by a discussion of strategies for making their work persuasive, for winning the reader's assent.

What distinguishes the rhetoric of poetry from the rhetoric of discursive prose, I argue here, is that its argument, in Aristotle's terms, is based more on *ethos* than on *logos,* more on the character of the speaker than on logical proof. For a poem to be convincing, the primary task of the writer is to construct a speaker whose company is worth keeping, who exhibits certain virtues that win the reader's sympathetic attention. The advice about craft in these essays is therefore advice about constructing convincing voices. This emphasis on the presence of a speaker standing behind the lines, one common to most traditional approaches to poetry, does not mean that my argument ignores the critique, often mounted today, of what is sometimes called "the Romantic ego." The voice of a speaker shut away from the world in his or her own subjectivity is only one of the many possible voices available to a writer. But my approach does inevitably lead me to disagree with certain skeptical positions common today that cast doubt on the possibility of creating any persuasive poetic voice, and this doubt deserves some attention.

For critics who embrace skeptical theory, any argument for the persuasive power of an individual poetic voice is based on two beliefs about the self that we now recognize to be fictions: that it is unified and that it is free. Against the notion that the self is a stable unity, these critics posit a loosely joined company of shifting qualities, closer to the self of Hume, say, than that of essentialist thinkers from Plato to Freud. To some extent this critique can serve as a useful reminder that the notion of self is an open concept, that many different kinds of selfhood are available. Though a self that is radically unstable and discontinuous would make any kind of deliberate thought impossible, the notion of a monolithic self, without any conflicts and uncertainties, may be equally unprofitable as a model for poetry. Surely we need to be flexible in defining the selfhood required for an individual voice to be distinctive. We ought not to exclude, for example, poetry that presents mental processes as fluid, that works by association rather than by logical, linear progression. So we would not want to pronounce as unpoetical the typical speaker in John Ashbery's work, who allows his observations, sensations, dreams, and memories to come together for brief moments of clarity and then dissolve and reassemble in fresh configurations. Ashbery's speaker may deliberately remove himself from the yearning Romantic voice that struggles against great odds to remake the world in the image of human desire; he may be content to witness the flow of experience rather than transform it. But his voice is still distinct, stable, and definite. In giving up Romantic projects Ashbery is not so much casting out the self as choosing one set of writerly virtues over another—irreverence toward tradition over respect, comedy over seriousness, irony over directness, unpredictability over linearity, an Ovidian embrace of mutability over a Virgilian nostalgia about what is passing away. But the voice that results is so distinctive that even a few lines betray its telltale tonalities.

The second critique of an approach that makes voice primary is that it presumes a speaker who is free, for only such a speaker can establish any authority. This presumption ignores, it is argued, all the historical forces that make what any speaker says determined by cultural conditioning. In a qualified way the truth of this skeptical position can't be denied. We are all shaped to some extent by the times we live in; we can never wholly escape the dominant vocabulary of the moment. But in its absolute form, which denies the possibility of any distancing at all of one's attitudes from one's world, which sees no significant difference between resistance and conformity, it is false to experience. All meaningful discussion of truthfulness in art is a discussion about degree, as even skeptics must tacitly acknowledge if their own writing is to have any point. They could not expect any reader to waste his time with their critique if he believed their arguments were merely an unconscious expression of a dominant ideology; and they would not waste their time seeking any reader's assent if the reader's settled beliefs have all been predetermined. To be consistent, these critics, who allow for themselves the possibility of standing back from their age in some limited way, must grant the same possibility to the artists who interest them. And unless they make such a concession, they cannot deal with one of the basic aesthetic questions, why some works of art are more enduring than others, why some outlast their times and their immediate audiences. The difference between ephemeral and lasting poetry has always been regarded in part as a function of the difference between a lazy acceptance of the clichés of the moment and a willingness to hold up all that one values to critical scrutiny. The success of this effort will never be more than partial. But abandoning the notion of the poet as the inspired announcer of timeless truth does not require embracing the notion that the poet is only the unconscious transmitter of cultural convention. If poets can't observe the earth from a heavenly platform or from the prophet's mountain, the view from even a garret window might still prove liberating. The need to work for distance is implicit in the traditional expectation that poets enter into dialogue with writers outside their own immediate society, inhabiting a second society of writers from a variety of times and places who are able to distance themselves to some extent from their own times. Of course one's choice of writers for this second society, and the virtues for which one admires them, is in part determined by one's own cultural inheritance. But writers who make the effort at dialogue are likelier to be freer of local prejudice than those who take as their models only their neighbors and their contemporaries.

Though much skeptical criticism can be faulted for its absolutism, for its conflating the limits to freedom with the absence of any freedom, it often performs a useful service in pointing out the ways in which our limited freedom is under constant threat. One of the goals of language poetry, for example, is to sharpen our awareness of how much of contemporary discourse has become so corrupted by the languages of political and commercial manipulation, by the argot of the hard-sell and the soft-sell, that it no longer functions as genuine communication. So these poets tend to make the surface of their poems opaque in order to suggest that the transparency of language is an illusion, forcing us to confront the ways in which the language we use in our daily lives distorts, conceals, and confuses. The liability of this emphasis, which suggests that any real communication must occur against the grain of typical usage, is that it may cede too much of the battleground to the enemy. In its suspicion of clarity, it tends to limit its task to the undermining of conventional discourse rather than trying to reclaim ordinary speech for truth-telling. As a result, it risks numbing the reader with a steady flow of irony. We may ask why the intelligence that is exhibited in the clear-eyed cataloging of linguistic abuses might not be used to help purify more directly the language of the tribe, resisting demotic speech by trying to say as clearly as possible what the poet believes to be important. Such efforts may at times seem naive, the symptom of a failure to understand the degree of one's own reliance on assumptions built into an inherited vocabulary. But all poets inherit a dominant discourse, and the poets we admire seem to be able to transform it into personal speech. If we choose, we can find clear links between Emily Dickinson's discourse and the discourse of nineteenth-century American Protestantism, or between Whitman's voice and that of American boosterism. But we can also see that these two writers reshaped the language they were given, creating distinctive speakers that still move and challenge us.

The very real threat to convincing personal speech that we must confront today is finally an argument not for abandoning the demand for such speech but for asserting the primacy of the speaker even more emphatically. In a time when the notion of "self" is under attack, when the demand for the speaker's presence seems a relic from the files of an outmoded Romanticism, it is important to reassert the peculiar value of poetry in making such a presence convincing. The central experience of reading a poem, this book contends, is that of making contact with a whole human being, not only with arguments and opinions but with a complex of emotional, ethical, and aesthetic attitudes expressed with the kind of directness and openness that we experience in the frank speech of a friend. The speaker, of course, may often bear a connection with the writer much less direct than the one presumed by some Romantics. Even Yeats, who called himself one of the "last romantics," criticized the notion of poetry as self-expression for offering too passive an account of the process of creation, for ignoring the fact that the speaker is a role that the writer deliberately fashions.[2] For Yeats this role is that of an ideal complement to the writer's natural self, a mask of fabricated personality that he imposes on his inherited character, with the poet's distinctive tonalities generated by the resulting conflict. For those of us with postmodern sensibilities, this formulation may seem to entail too restrictive a notion of role-playing because it gives a privileged status to only one set of natural dispositions and one ideal other. But Yeats would probably reply that a writer's individual voices, however various they may be, will usually display a family likeness, and this common element may be only partly a matter of choice. In any case, I agree with Yeats's premise that what matters most in a poem is the constructed voice, the "personality" that adopts a particular perspective and invites the reader to engage with it. No matter what existential state writers bring to their writing, however incoherent, chaotic, or empty they may feel, in the act of writing they take on, at least provisionally, a clear perspective, a definite point of view, which is embodied in a speaker capable of winning the reader's sympathetic appreciation. To this extent the writer, as writer, always speaks from strength, not from weakness. Poets as individuals may be no more ready than anyone else to follow Nietzsche's pronouncement in *The Gay Science* that "one thing is needful, to give style to one's character."[3] But when they sit down to write they work to give style to a voice.

The notion that poets speak from strength is akin to the traditional notion that the inspiration of poets comes from within as much as from without, a notion that in America has received its most radical formulation by Emerson. We may have trouble accepting Emerson's insistence that the poet must "leave the world" and "not know any longer the times, customs, graces, politics, or opinions of men, but . . . take all from the muse"; but beneath this hyperbole lies a pragmatic observation about the poetic voice, that it does not convince unless it seems to be the result of original and solitary reflection rather than the result of the sifting and rearranging of received ideas. For Emerson the originality thus achieved allows the poet to connect more deeply with the reader. It expresses itself in a voice that is more deeply representative of the whole human personality, that has not allowed too much of itself to be smoothed away in order to work without friction within the accepted notions of social life. Though we may be gloomier than Emerson about the distance we can stand from the shared conventions of the moment, as readers we are soon bored with writers who accept those conventions without a struggle, and as writers we would rather be classed with Emerson's rough-mannered, challenging bard than with the "lyrist" who merely tries to be charming.[4]

My emphasis on the presentation of a strong-voiced, independent speaker inevitably puts my approach at odds not only with skepticism about the coherence and freedom of any self but also with skepticism about the claims of any text, as text, to be more than a self-enclosed system of reference, to make any contact at all with the world. This view of literature has some validity if we define "the world" as what is eternally valid, what is true in an absolute sense, but the world that literature tries to throw light on is not that of ultimate being but that of common human experience. And here literature has as much claim as other modes of understanding, particularly because its conclusions are grounded in concrete situations. It is true that our understanding of any particular work is enlarged by our knowledge of other works like it, that all literature works by conventions of representation. No one would deny, for example, that the figures of tragedy and epic behave more nobly than most people in ordinary life, with their powers of articulation undiminished at moments of crisis that would reduce most of us to silence. But for us to comprehend what they say and be moved by it, we have to understand them not merely by the rules of literary convention but also by our own notions of appropriateness to the occasion, notions that we bring to the work from the world of experience. With regard to speakers in poems, we understand their statements the same way we understand the speech of people around us, though the poem is more self-contained, unable to depend on a context of other conversations with the speaker to supply essential information. A poem does make some claims that distinguish it from ordinary speech, including the claim that it will possess enough vividness and coherence and relevance to make the reader want to return to it, but this claim does not involve the promise of contact with an ultimate reality, only of contact with a speaker whose discourse the reader finds engaging and revealing.

I do not want to dismiss the efforts of those poets who, prompted by a concern with the dangers of claiming too much for art, write poems that accentuate the artifice of the genre, who find ways to foreground technique in order to suggest how methods determine meaning, building into their work contradictions that make implications indeterminate. But I do want to point out that to focus primarily on exposing the distance between art and life is to confine oneself to a minor form of writing, to reduce the writer's work to a cautionary role. It means turning away from the opportunity that the most ambitious art provides its audience, the chance to have one's own vision of life challenged and enlarged. And even if this kind of skeptical poem can avoid sounding narrow, it may sound evasive. If the determined deconstruction of meaning suggests, at first, the license of play, it may sound at last like the writer's ingenious attempts to escape responsibility for any perspective the work appears to imply. Accused of telling lies, the writer can always blame the limitations of language, or point to the subtle subversions of overt meaning, or insist that what the reader has taken as a comment on life is only a tissue of references to other texts. A theory that tries to disengage the work completely from the world runs the risk of fostering speakers whose *ethos* is suspect, who sound as if they don't want to commit themselves to a clear point of view.

Separating art from life not only suggests that poetry doesn't matter; it also leads to the notion that poetry is deceitful. The supposed greatness of a great work gets reduced to its great success in misleading its audience, to its power to seduce its readers into believing that the work can tell them something about the way things really are. And this skeptical attempt to demythologize the work leads to the mythologizing of the act of reading. Good readers, this approach implies, are not those, as tradition would have it, who are most open to the work but those least likely to be taken in. They are able to move through a book as the heroes of romance move though a haunted forest where the trees are full of poisoned fruit and the paths full of deadly shape-shifters disguised as beautiful maidens. Arming themselves against temptation, they succeed in their quests by proving themselves unshaken and unseduced by all they encounter. This view of the poet as a dark enchanter and the reader as Sir Galahad, though full of high drama, has very little to do with the actual relation of a serious writer and an enlightened reader. Persuasive poetry is not founded on the premise of the reader's naiveté. Though poets expect their readers to make "the willing suspension of disbelief" that Coleridge speaks of as the prerequisite for aesthetic engagement, they don't want readers who are uncritical. They know in fact that the relation of the work to the reader is a very delicate one, which one false move on the author's part—one phrase, say, that seems meant to advertise the poet rather than serve the poem—immediately jeopardizes. Such fragility makes a book like this one, which attempts to make writers more sensitive to the implications of their rhetoric, potentially useful.

While at odds with skeptical theory, my approach is in harmony with most approaches that regard the work as the product of conscious choices, including most thematic studies, and in particular with the kind of pragmatic rhetorical tradition that relates these choices to their effects on the reader. Some of the most useful recent rhetorical criticism has approached the poem as a dramatic event in which a fictive speaker performs a speech act that gives specific embodiment to one or more of the basic tasks we ask ordinary speech to perform—explaining, questioning, demanding, promising, apologizing, praising, castigating, and the like. Only some of these speech acts imply a fictive listener, but all imply an audience that witnesses the performance. The social nature of the activity asked of the reader by this dramatic model has been well expressed by Richard Ohmann, who argues that works of literature "invite the reader to participate in the imaginative construction of a world—or at least as much of one that is necessary to give the speech acts an adequate setting." [5] A full description of this imaginative participation has to allow room, as Charles Altieri points out, both for the direct engagement we feel with the poetic utterance—with our willingness to enter the situation and identify with the speaker—and for the distance we require for reflecting on the way the formal properties of the poem help control our responses to the speaker, define the necessary context for understanding, and help us relate the specifics of the poem to the world outside.[6] I would like to think that I have defined the argument from *ethos* in a way that does justice to these aspects of the poem while maintaining a practical focus, concentrating on those aspects of character that need to be enacted for a speech act to be persuasive and on the specific techniques that help make the enactment possible.

The rhetorical critic whose emphasis on *ethos* is perhaps closest to my own is Wayne Booth, particularly in his *The Company We Keep: An Ethics of Fiction,* which defines the appeal of a work of literature through the metaphor of friendship, the reader responding to the successful work as to a friend whose company is sought for its own sake, from a sense of shared attitudes toward life.[7] In writing a book on the ethical effects of reading prose fiction, Booth is less concerned with the strategies of ethical argument than he is with showing the ways in which our emotional engagement with a work is related to the choice of the kind of person we wish to be. But the metaphor he introduces is perhaps even more appropriate for poetry than it is for fiction, for in a poem we seem invited to enter into a direct relation with the speaker, without the indirection of a mediating narrative.

The one application of a pragmatic view of poetry with which I find myself in only partial sympathy is the one influenced by theories of multiculturalism. My problem here is that this perspective can be formulated with either expansive or restrictive implications. In its expansive mode it urges us to enlarge our notions of relevant art by engaging with work that is often labeled as marginal or peripheral to our culture, arguing that such work may in fact turn out to appeal to us more strongly than work that has traditionally been regarded as central to the canon. In the restrictive formulation of multiculturalism, on the other hand, the appeal of any work is limited by the essential disunity of human experience, by its being made up of a multitude of separate, irreconcilable perspectives, each defined and determined primarily by inherited membership in a particular group, whether gender, race, tribe, nationality, or social class. To learn to speak as a member of a group to other members of the group is thus the first task for any writer. I resist this essentialist formulation not only because it restricts a writer's freedom to choose his or her own set of primary loyalties but also because I think it leads to unconvincing poetry. I agree with Emerson that the voice that convinces is the voice of an individual, the voice of a speaker who persuades us that he has not accepted his notions ready-made from others but has figured out what he believes on his own. The speaker who presents himself as a spokesperson for a "we" leaves his readers wondering how much of himself he has had to suppress in order to take on this collective identity. In place of this notion of identity as membership, I would substitute the notion of the individual implied by the nonrestrictive version of multiculturalism, an individual whose concerns, however peripheral they may appear in terms of conventional rubrics, are large enough to be representative. "To believe your own thought, to believe that what is true for you in your private heart is true for all men— that is genius," Emerson boldly declares. And though we might want to remove any possibility of a restrictive reading by deleting the word "men," his insight here is crucial. Great writing begins when writers see their experience as primary, not secondary, universal in application, not limited in relevance to one group or another.

"All men" may rightly be regarded by some writers as too vague an audience to inspire much effort. They may find it more useful to write for a selection of individuals. But if this selection is too narrowly conceived, if it is reducible to members of a few easily labeled constituencies, the work is liable to be parochial. Perhaps the best way for writers to address an audience that is both immediate and open is to imagine a single person endowed with unrestricted powers of sympathy and discrimination. This individual is in good part a fiction, but a fiction likely to have liberating results. In this regard I want to quote a passage from Emerson's *Journals* on the best audience for a writer: "Happy is he who looks only into his work to know if it will succeed, never into the times or the public opinion; and who writes from the love of imparting certain thoughts and not from the necessity of sale—who writes always to *the unknown friend.*" "Friend," not friends, because the reader, like the writer, has not submerged his or her individuality in a corporation. "Unknown," not known, and so not able to be defined in terms of place and class, nature or nurture, that might offer the writer some easy basis of appeal. This is the reader who can't be fooled when the world is fooled, the reader most likely to keep us honest and so most likely to guarantee that our work will still be of interest long after its local occasions have ceased to matter.

In attempting to answer the question how to create a voice that might convince this ideal reader, the reader we would like to be and to write for, I begin, in the first chapter, by defining what I take to be the virtues that all poetic voices must exhibit in order to be convincing, and in subsequent chapters I discuss particular strategies for enacting those virtues in ways that make the voice seem open and expansive rather than dogmatic and restrictive. Chapters 2 and 3 focus on the two rhetorical decisions that most directly control the speaker's distance in a poem, choice of grammatical person (first, second, or third) and the use of irony, and try to show how the speaker's tone is in part a function of the virtues that the writer wants the speaker to exemplify. The three essays that follow deal with strategies for expanding the reach of a poem—into public life, into narratives of psychic change, and into mythical reference—without sounding overreaching. And in the final chapter I return to the basic supposition of this study, that the speaker must convincingly present himself as a free agent, and discuss how a speaker can admit limitations in knowledge and power without presenting himself as a victim who is allowed no significant choices.

My method of argument is the traditional one of example. Though I use a few bad examples, I concentrate on what I consider models of rhetorical skill because in writing one learns mainly by imitation, not by avoidance. Most of my examples are in English, and most of these are American, written primarily in this century. But I make an effort to refer to the work of Whitman or Dickinson in almost every chapter, partly because they are still the two great influences on contemporary American poetry and partly because their obvious antinomies suggest that any single period can give rise to a range of discourses among which poets can choose as they work to discover and develop their own voices.

CHAPTER ONE

The Voice of Authority

MY ASSERTION in the introduction that the persuasiveness of a poem depends on the presence of a definite speaker with a sharply defined point of view is not intended to imply that the most confident-sounding speaker is always the most persuasive. The skeptical criticism that I have tried to answer briefly is an extreme form of a more qualified skepticism that makes many readers today feel more at home with a speaker's doubts than with his assurances, to be put off by any suggestion of smugness or swagger. Suspicious of self-proclaimed prophets, we want our poetic voices to show us that they don't claim to know all things, that they realize that all efforts to tell the truth are more likely to be expressions of the particular needs of the truth-seeker than revelations of the real nature of the world. What we find to be true, we all tend to agree, is what is most helpful in promoting the conditions that best serve our interests. And even if we define these interests in large and generous ways, not in small and mean ones, we want to be reminded not to claim as true for others what in fact is true only for ourselves and for people like us.

Poetry is particularly suited to this task because it does not try to deny its subjective origins. The voices of poetry are particular, the speeches of particular characters in particular situations, and the meaning of what is said is never intended to be completely separable

from its context. In narrative and dramatic poetry the context is immediately apparent in terms of plot, setting, and character. In poems
spoken in the first person by an "I" not always easy to distinguish
from the writer, the kind of poem most commonly written today, the
context may be less obvious; but some particular occasion is almost
always suggested, and the speaker's mood is clearly implied. We read
such a poem to make contact not so much with some objective truth
but with a particular mind trying to know what is true for it, a contact more immediate than the kind we are likely to get in fiction and
drama. And if a speaker claims to be totally objective and favors abstract, categorical pronouncements, we are likely to find his or her
work unconvincing.

But our demand that speakers acknowledge their personal focus
coexists with a counterdemand, one that I think is just as basic for
serious readers of poetry: that the voices we meet in poems try to
make sense of experience. Though the truth of the poem is particular,
the speaker needs to make us believe that his concerns are representative, that his efforts to clarify life for himself will be useful to others.
Any display of bias must therefore be accompanied by an awareness
of the bias and an effort to counteract it. In this regard a great narrative poet like Homer can serve as a model for the writer of a first-
person poem with a personal focus. As a Greek, Homer may naturally
favor the side of his ancestors, the Achaeans, in the Trojan War, but
as a poet he does his best to treat the Trojan heroes with sympathy.
And though his loyalties are to the fighting and dying mortals, not to
the immortal Olympians, he does his best to imagine how the war
might look from an immortal perspective, so that he is both involved
and removed from the action. We cannot say that Homer's treatment
of the war is true to some absolute reality, only that he has done justice to the material he has chosen, that he has explored it with a rich-
ness that makes his poem still moving long after the particular audience for which it was written, whatever its biases, has ceased to exist.

Because of the smaller compass of the first-person poem, its authority usually results less from the slow building up of particular perceptions than from the direct presenting of a character we can trust. In terms of traditional rhetoric, we can say, as suggested in the introduction, that the argument of the first-person poem is primarily an ethical argument, based on the *ethos* or moral qualities exhibited by the speaker, and only secondarily an appeal to particular evidence. To examine the source of authority in such poems, then, is to examine the qualities we can expect to find in speakers who prove convincing. No two speakers, to be sure, are exactly alike; and for most practical criticism it is more useful to concentrate on what distinguishes one speaker from another, including speakers created by the same writer, than to ask what all convincing speakers share. The larger question is harder to answer because it is based on an almost unlimited universe of discourse, all the persuasive poems ever written; but it needs to be addressed if we are to understand how authority in a poem is established.

What virtues, then, must a speaker display if his words are to have authority? For me, three are fundamental—passion, discrimination, and inclusiveness. That is, the speaker must show, first, that he cares about what he is saying; second, that he has reached his position not by ignoring opposed positions but by considering them and finding them wanting; and third, that he sees the connections between the subject immediately at hand and other issues. Taking them in turn, I want to discuss some of the ways these qualities are embodied in poetic form.

To seem passionate the speaker must give the impression that his words express a deep-seated conviction, that he stands behind what he is saying. If he is to convince us that what he is saying is true for us, his first task is to convince us it is true for him. The most important technical means that poets have at their disposal to communicate conviction is rhythm, if we define the term broadly to include not only the formal or informal pattern of stressed and unstressed syllables but all that is involved in thinking in lines as well as in sentences. Used well, rhythm makes us feel the presence of a speaker behind the words. Even a poem of two lines may provide enough space for a poet sensitive to the stresses and pauses of his syntax to create a voice of deep conviction. Consider this couplet that Ben Jonson uses as a preface for his book of epigrams:

> Pray thee, take care, that tak'st my book in hand
> To read it well, that is, to understand.[1]

These lines are an appeal for Jonson's book to be read with careful attention. To be effective they have to suggest that they themselves deserve careful attention. In this they succeed, despite their plainness, partly because their meaning keeps expanding. What opens as a plea shifts suddenly, in the second foot, to cautionary advice and then, in the second line, to formal instruction as the poet defines what reading well really means. In quick succession the speaker is suitor, enjoiner, and moral instructor. What needs to be noticed here is how much our sense of the speaker's presence is dependent on the prosody, on the handling of rhythm and syntax. The poem opens abruptly with a spondee, "Pray thee," not with the expected iamb of the heroic couplet, and the abruptness suggests that the speaker has dispensed with the language of formal petition for plain directness. The line is then disrupted even more emphatically by the unexpected spondee of the second foot, "take care," which underscores the shift from plea to warning, and our sense of the poem's irregularity is deepened by the enjambment of the first line, which keeps the meaning of the advice suspended to the middle of the second line. The strong break here emphatically isolates the crucial definition that concludes the poem, and the caesura within this final half-line gives so much weight to the final word, "understand," that the reader is forced to reconsider its meaning. Someone, we feel, is talking to us here, someone not interested in writing a formal couplet but in using the form to say something of importance. How crucial a part the prosody plays in establishing the speaker's emphatic presence becomes clear if we rewrite the poem to make the syntax and rhythms more regular:

> Who'er thou art that tak'st my book in hand
> Take care to read it well and understand.

By removing the spondees and the caesurae we have lost the speaker. The singsong iambs give us no personal emphasis. The rhythm seems dictated entirely by the form, not by the pressure of the poet's concern. What tone we can hear seems neutral, almost flippant. We are being asked to care about a book by a speaker who displays none of the concern that Jonson's syntax substantiates.

Developing a passionate syntax was important for Jonson because he wanted to move his poetry beyond the private concerns of the Elizabethan love lyric to concentrate on issues of general social significance. To be as convincing an authority on public morals as on the state of his own heart, he tried to bring into his poetry the presence of a concrete, individual voice that he found in Roman writers like Horace and Martial. In this effort he has served as a model for many poets, in his time and ours, Yeats perhaps most notably, who reaches in some of his late poems for the largest generalizations while managing to maintain a passionate presence. Consider the familiar opening couplets of "The Second Coming," which have as their subject nothing less than the breakdown of Western civilization:

> Turning and turning in the widening gyre
> The falcon cannot hear the falconer;
> Things fall apart; the centre cannot hold;
> Mere anarchy is loosed upon the world,
> The blood-dimmed tide is loosed, and everywhere
> The ceremony of innocence is drowned;
> The best lack all conviction, while the worst
> Are full of passionate intensity.[2]

Doubtless part of the power of these lines resides in the suggestiveness of the images: the wheeling falcon, whose own natural energies are no longer controlled by its master, as if the traditional disciplines of culture are no longer effective; the man-made object that begins to crumble at the edges under the stress of outward pressure; the blood-colored sea loosed upon civilization like a wild animal. But to see how much the intensity of these lines is in great part a function of their rhythm, we have only to rewrite the passage in regular iambic pentameter:

> The falcon turns and turns in a wider gyre.
> He cannot hear the cry of the falconer.
> Things break because the center cannot hold.
> Mere anarchy is let loose on the world.
> The tide that's dimmed by blood is loosed.
> The ritual of innocence is drowned.
> The best have lost their firm convictions.
> The worst are full of fierce intensity.

Because of Yeats's variations from the iambic, his speaker seems much more responsive than the speaker of the rewrite to the implications of what is actually being described. The falcon of his first line moves much more quickly and wildly, the stresses more emphatic because more separated by unstressed syllables. The falling apart of the objects he describes is underscored by the median break of the line. His anarchy, in line 4, is "loos'd" more emphatically as we rush so quickly over the unstressed syllables that a foot seems to drop away. His "blood-dimmed tide" gets the weight of three bunched stresses to suggest its power. His weak-willed "best" are allowed only part of a line, not a whole line that would balance the worst, and the stresses in the last line on the words "passionate" and "intensity" are so heavy on the first stressed syllables that the second stresses are muted. The emphatic rhythms of Yeats's speaker make clear the passionate nature of his response to the magnitude of the collapse he is witnessing, and this passion is crucial in qualifying the dichotomy of the final lines. The "worst" are not the only ones capable of passionate intensity after all. But the speaker of the rewrite describes the collapse in so quiet and plodding a monotone that we have to conclude either that he does not believe what he is saying or that he is emotionally torpid.

The important role played by rhythm in making a poem convincing may give pause to those who believe that a poet should be seriously engaged in clarifying experience. It may suggest, at first at least, that a poem is less a matter of truth-telling than of manipulating the reader. The poet seems a master of illusion, a showman who uses the smoke and mirrors of technique to make weak arguments appear stronger. We might respond to this objection the way the Sophists responded to Socrates' criticism that they taught the art of persuasion and not the art of seeking the truth: namely, that rhetoric is a tool, and the fact that it may be misused by liars should not keep truth-tellers from using it to make the truth convincing. But a deeper problem with the objection is that it seems to be based on a false opposition between style and content. Rhythm is not an adornment of a statement but one of its elements. It shapes it, giving it focus and clarity. It endows it with a specific weight that helps define its value. The falcons of Yeats's poem are not dressed-up versions of the falcons in the rewrite. They are different creatures, inherently more graceful and powerful, and their inability to hear the falconer has therefore much deeper implications. And the speaker of Yeats's poem is not a more energetic version of the speaker in the rewrite. He represents a different sensibility, one capable of responding with the feeling the situation demands. The issue here is that of decorum. Yeats's rhythms are appropriate to their subject. The rhythms of the rewrite are not.

They deny the importance of what the poem claims to be important. Their flaw may be called the flaw of bathos or unintended deflation, in contrast to the opposite flaw of overwriting or inflation, in which the rhythms of a poem are more charged and portentous than the subject requires. In either case the truth of the material has been violated.

If the speaker can convince us that he means what he says, that he is speaking from passionate conviction, not glibly or half-heartedly, he still won't be convincing unless we trust his judgment. We call a speaker judicious or discriminating if we feel that the opinions he or she expresses are reached after considering alternative opinions. Without this quality, the passionate voice will sound naive. So in Jonson's preface, the speaker's plea for understanding works on a distinction between ordinary casual reading and a deeper kind of engagement. The speaker in Yeats's poem is much more emotionally aroused, and he does not contrast his vision of the age to other visions. He simply presents images of the breakdown in a way that makes them seem directly witnessed and so incontrovertible. And yet we feel the speaker is discriminating because he is detached enough, even as he witnesses the collapse, to view it not as a unique event but as the outgrowth of possibilities latent in the preceding order. The falcon that used to fly still flies and the falconer still calls, but now they can no longer make contact. The center, which has always been able to hold the edges, still makes the effort, but now it fails. The tide has always been dimmed by blood, waiting to drown innocence, and now it's free to do so. The best and worst have always been with us, though now the best have lost their self-confidence and the worst have strengthened theirs. In suggesting how the seeds of disorder live within civilization, the lines make clear how fragile every order must be and so broaden the implications of the vision.

The most dramatic way to confront opposed positions is to have the speaker directly address an opponent and argue him or her into concession. This is the strategy that John Donne uses to give new life to the Renaissance love poem. His idealistic poems make claims for the importance of love that are more radical than the traditional poem of plea and complaint, but his speakers can't be patronized as self-absorbed because they confront those who would disparage love and argue them down. So in "The Canonization," in a tone that is by turns angry, mocking, riddling, and pedantic, the speaker turns on an auditor who has accused love of being a childish pastime and exposes the emptiness of the worldly life the auditor is committed to. But argumentative structure needn't involve an imagined auditor. It is present to some extent whenever a speaker defines his or her position through contrast with another, a mode that is central to many poems we may not regard as obviously dramatic. We think of Emily Dickinson's speaker, for example, as essentially private, the voice of inner joy and agonies; but one of the traits that makes this voice distinctive is her willingness to defend her circumscription, to make it clear that she turns from the public world not to escape its pressures but to concern herself with life on a deeper and more challenging level:

> To fight aloud, is very brave—
> But *gallanter*, I know
> Who charge within the bosom
> The Cavalry of Wo—
>
> Who win, and nations do not see—
> Who fall—and none observe—
> Whose dying eyes, no Country
> Regards with patriot love—
>
> We trust, in plumed procession
> For such, the Angels go—
> Rank after Rank, with even feet—
> And Uniforms of Snow.[3]

The speaker here not only asserts that inner struggles entail more courage than outer ones but also indirectly attacks the values the world lives by. She borrows military metaphors to endow the inner life with glory, but finally suggests that such figures are part of a world of public causes and rewards that cannot do justice to the deeper significance of individual success and failure. Even the heaven imagined by the group mind fails to be spiritual. Its angels are all company angels, and so can give only cold comfort to a soul scarred by solitary trials. Through a bold argument indirectly stated, the speaker affirms the reality of the invisible world and the fictitiousness of the visible one.

In poets who avoid this kind of direct opposition, it may sometimes be hard to find any position that is being repudiated. An imagistic poem by Williams, for example, that attempts to seize a passing moment before it vanishes, seems to share very little with Dickinson's challenging assertions. But even here, other modes of seeing may be indirectly criticized. Consider "Proletarian Portrait":

> A big young bareheaded woman
> in an apron
>
> Her hair slicked back standing
> on the street
>
> One stockinged foot toeing
> the sidewalk
>
> Her shoe in her hand. Looking
> intently into it
>
> She pulls out the paper insole
> to find the nail
>
> That has been hurting her [4]

This poem is a snapshot of an ordinary, passing moment saved from oblivion by the camera of the poet. The scene is worth remembering, presumably, because of the woman's healthy vigor and lack of self-consciousness. She has an earthy energy and nonchalance. But the title of the poem encourages us to widen the context of the description by contrasting the hardiness and innocence of the servant girl with the delicacy and sophistication of a lady who might be more typically presented in the genre of the portrait. The point here is not to replace aristocratic notions of beauty with proletarian, but to suggest that our notions of beauty have to be large enough to find examples on the street as well as in protected interiors. The young servant looking for a nail in her shoe is a far cry from the princess who proves her noble blood by being able to feel a pea through seven mattresses. But she has her own grace as she toes the sidewalk, and in curing her own pain she suggests she is far more equipped than the hypersensitive princess of fairy tale for the ordinary world. The poem works, then, without any overt discriminations, but indirectly pits one aesthetic against another.

One of the most significant challenges in American poetry to the notion that the authority of the speaker depends in part on an ability to anticipate opposed positions can be found in the accomplishment of some of the more expansive poems in *Leaves of Grass*. Whitman's speaker in "Song of Myself," for example, writes as if he is looking at the world for the first time and celebrates all he sees through a vivid listing, not by arguing. But behind the speaker's praise of the relentlessly commonplace and homely lies a judgment about the practice of his contemporary poets, which suffers, in his eyes, from too narrow a notion of the beautiful:

> And limitless are leaves stiff or drooping in the fields,
> And brown ants in the little wells beneath them,
> And mossy scabs of the worm fence, heap'd stones, elder,
>   mullein and poke-weed.

It's easy to praise sunsets and daffodils. It's hard to praise ants and weeds and mossy scabs. Until included here, they had in fact been excluded from poetry in English. We can't, to be sure, call the speaker of this poem critical or confrontational in any ordinary sense. The stylistic device we think of as peculiarly his, the catalog, is meant to suggest not only the rich variety of the world and the uniqueness of each particular but the ultimate equality of all things. Each fact is equally complete and "limitless." But this assertion of equality involves a critique of traditional systems of value, a critique that periodically surfaces as the "Walt Whitman" of the poem juxtaposes various scenes that social convention would regard as radically different:

> The bride unrumples her white dress, the minute-hand of the
>   clock moves slowly,
> The opium-eater reclines with rigid head and just-open'd lips,
> The prostitute draggles her shawl, her bonnet bobs on her tipsy
>   and pimpled neck,
> The crowd laugh at her blackguard oaths, the men jeer and
>   wink to each other,
> (Miserable! I do not laugh at your oaths or jeer you;)
> The President holding a cabinet council is surrounded by the
>   great Secretaries,
> On the piazza walk three matrons stately and friendly with
>   twined arms,
> The crew of the fish-smack pack repeated layers of halibut in
>   the hold.[5]

In deliberately linking bride, prostitute, stately matrons, President, and crew of the fish-smack, the speaker aggressively juxtaposes his leveling values with those of traditional hierarchies. The speaker wins authority by making clear he is fully aware of what his view of the world repudiates.

In all these examples of critical response, the opposed position is external to the speaker, and the speaker's authority is enhanced by showing us that he has been able to anticipate objections. But in many poems the objection is internal and the poem can be viewed as a dialogue between two parts of the self. We may think of this kind of poetry as particularly common since the Romantics, an expression of the shift from Augustan, pragmatic poetics focused on the audience to Romantic, expressive poetics focused on the poet; but the genre reaches back to the beginnings of lyric poetry. When Catullus writes *"Odi et amo,"* I hate and I love, he is already working in a tradition of erotic ambivalence. And early Christian poems about the war between sin and virtue are as direct a model as any Romantic poem for a poem like Yeats's "Dialogue of Self and Soul." What is new about the Romantic poem of inner dialogue is that the opposed voices are presented sequentially as different stages in the speaker's development. The poems are structured as narratives, not as arguments, and often, as in Coleridge's conversation poems, the narrative is not placed in the past but enacted in the present as the poet moves by a process of association from one state to another, typically from ignorance to insight and uneasiness to rest. For many poets today this kind of plot is a particularly useful strategy for satisfying the skeptical demands of their readers and themselves for modest speakers, for voices that make it clear that their conclusions are not meant as final and fixed pronouncements but as the status report of a process that involves much groping and confusion.

Whereas the Romantic narrative of psychic change is based on a faith in the mind's own healing powers, in contemporary poetry the change is more likely to be simply a movement toward a deeper understanding of the subject at hand. The speaker begins his poem in doubt about the import of his experience and then discovers gradually what he believes. Lowell's "Alfred Corning Clark" is a good example of the genre:

> You read the *New York Times*
> every day at recess,

but in its dry
obituary, a list
of your wives, nothing is news,
except the ninety-five
thousand dollar engagement ring
you gave the sixth.
Poor rich boy,
you were unreasonably adult
at taking your time,
and died at forty-five.
Poor Al Clark,
behind your enlarged,
hardly recognizable photograph,
I feel the pain.
You were alive. You are dead.

You wore bow-ties and dark
blue coats, and sucked
wintergreen or cinnamon lifesavers
to sweeten your breath.
There must be something—
some one to praise
your triumphant diffidence,
your refusal of exertion,
the intelligence
that pulsed in the sensitive,
pale concavities of your forehead.
You never worked,
and were third in the form.
I owe you something—
I was befogged,
and you were too bored,

quick and cool to laugh.
You are dear to me, Alfred;
our reluctant souls united
in our unconventional
illegal games of chess
on the St. Mark's quadrangle.
You usually won—
motionless
as a lizard in the sun.[6]

The speaker has chosen a difficult subject for an elegy. Clark's life was uninspiring, if not tawdry, and his association with the poet neither long nor deep. Though the poem opens with a dismissal of the sensationalistic perspective of the *Times,* the poet's own attitude toward Clark is initially patronizing, summarizing the early waste of Clark's life with the witty and distant "you were unreasonably adult / at taking your time." But the poet soon makes it clear that he wants to be as sympathetic as he can, and much of the interest of the poem lies in its dramatizing the poet's moving from detachment to involvement, a process whose stages are marked by the shifting of names, from the formal full name of the title, to the witty typecasting of "Poor rich boy," to the tender and particular "Poor Al Clark," to the intimate "Alfred." The first movement past irony comes with the recognition that Clark's death involves the loss of possibility that any death entails: "You were alive. You are dead." The next, more difficult step, as the poet tries to fix the particulars of appearance he still remembers clearly, is to find some quality in Clark to praise. The virtues singled out are based on negations, not really virtues at all, but they have a positive meaning for the speaker, whose childhood solitude was comforted by the presence of Clark's example of eccentric independence and nonchalance. The closing figure of the motionless lizard basking in the sun is not honorific in any traditional way, but it entails a respect for Clark's self-chosen separateness that underscores the distance the poet has moved from the patronizing irony with which he begins. In terms of the speaker's *ethos*, we can say that his powers of discrimination are supported here by the dramatization of his humility. By his confessing at the outset to his having no clear sense of how to proceed, by his willingness to show us his groping toward definition, we are made to feel that he regards his poem as a kind of clumsy substitute for a formal elegy, the best he can do, but not the best of its kind.

Readers who work with an expressivist view of poetry are especially likely to find poems of inner dialogue more authoritative than poems in which the speaker confronts others. Quarreling with others, they may say with Yeats, is rhetoric; quarreling with oneself is poetry. But readers who are suspicious of an expressivist view, who see it either as misguided about the centrality of voice or as promoting certain Romantic kinds of self-absorption, are likely to find this kind of poem particularly suspect, its rhetoric more manipulative because more indirect and ingratiating. With regard to Lowell's poem, they might argue that the humility enacted here is only a mask for the self-involved displacing of the subject of the poem from Clark's life to the speaker's problems in writing an elegy. I think the best way to answer such a critique is to admit that poems in this mode sometimes do go wrong, as they do in other modes, and then to point out that when they do the problem does not lie in the mode itself, in the speaker's choosing to present himself as divided and self-reflective, but in the speaker's displaying certain other traits of character that seem to restrict his handling of his problems. So I would agree that there is a rhetorical weakness in "Alfred Corning Clark" but would contend that it does not lie in the speaker's turning to the difficulties of writing an elegy but in his seeming to evade some of those difficulties, in his moving away from Clark's adult life to the small part of his childhood that the poet remembers. The "poor rich boy" of the opening, who dies at forty-five, is not integrated with the cool, detached chess player. He is merely set aside as irrelevant to the poet's real concern, commemorating the chess player's influence on the young poet. It is not Clark that is "dear" to the poet after all, only the "Alfred" that Clark once was, and only because Clark helped the poet inadvertently in a time of need. The poet is grateful for the help, but not grateful enough to try making sense of Clark's life as a whole. If the response of the *Times* to Clark is superficial, the poet's response, then, is partial and self-centered. The concluding figure is especially troubling. We think of metaphor as one of a writer's primary tools in reaching out beyond his subject or binding the disparate elements of a subject together. But this figure, instead of integrating Clark's life, insists on its disunity. What could be farther from the rich boy desperately seeking affection than the lizard at ease with itself, basking in the sun? And why, we wonder, isn't the poet interested in exploring the discrepancy?

Our sense that the response of Lowell's speaker here is too small for the occasion, too narrowly personal, leads us to the third demand that we make for authority in a poetic voice, the demand for inclusiveness. The speaker needs to make us believe that he is doing his subject justice, that in relating it to himself he is also relating it to the world. In fairness to Lowell, we should keep in mind that his best poems are models of the way in which a speaker can move out from private loss to embrace the largest issues. "For the Union Dead," for example, which begins as personal retrospection about the poet's boyhood daydreams at the Boston Aquarium, turns into a bitter indictment of contemporary American culture from a large, historical perspective. But for a poem to possess inclusiveness the movement need not be so obvious or so grand. All the poems we have dealt with here turn outward to some extent to engage their audience. Jonson's preface to his epigrams appeals directly for attention with the proud claim that his book will teach its readers something important. Whitman's cosmic bard celebrates the self by celebrating the world. The images used by Yeats's poet at the opening of "The Second Coming" keep the range of reference as wide as possible so that the collapse described does not seem grounded in any particular loss to the speaker, or to his family, or even to his country, but in a more fundamental historical reality. And the speaker of Emily Dickinson's poem on the superior courage of the inner struggle does not ground her argument in an appeal to her private experience. She speaks for everyone in a voice that is movingly impersonal, as if she has moved beyond private pain to a long-considered wisdom about the human condition.

Though inclusiveness involves, in its most basic form, avoiding too narrow or too private a treatment of the subject, in its more ambitious form it entails attempting to connect a wide range of apparently unrelated elements. The inclusive speaker presents himself as a seeker of unity amid diversity, and so gives expression to what the Romantics might call the synthesizing power of the imagination. The nearest examples of poets inspired by this kind of ambition are the great moderns, Yeats, Pound, and Eliot, who attempt to bring to bear on the moment a large, historical perspective that involves evaluating the entire sweep of Western culture. Their example, however, no longer seems to exert a deep influence. The moderns tended to be system-builders, and system-building has become suspect because so many of the particular horrors of the twentieth century seem attributable to the efforts of authoritarian ideologies to impose their single visions on the world. It may be unfair to allow a hatred of dogmatic political ideology to infect our respect for ambitious art, whose authority is earned and not imposed, and whose influence works toward widening our sympathies, not narrowing them. But the ease with which nations betrayed the values of their art has suggested to many that the influence and authority of art are not dependable, and art that makes grand claims for its own importance is particularly suspect. Humility has its excesses as well as ambition, however, and a distrust of system-building need not lead to a distrust of inclusiveness, though it may lead to more tentative and provisional conclusions. Poets should be able to write about all that interests them, and if their interests do not engage them deeply and widely in contemporary life, their poetry is likely to be thin. In traditional poetry the range of interests is expressed through a range of genres—epic, satire, epistle, epigram, georgic, pastoral, ode, and song. Though cultural change has undermined some of the assumptions that made these genres work, the communal impulses behind them are still alive, and all should find refuge within an enlarged version of the first-person poem.

One kind of inclusiveness common now is the rendering of the flow of ordinary life as opposed to reaching for a privileged moment of revelation. The speaker of this kind of poem has no grand mission or message. He is not burdened with any frustrated longings for the ideal that would interfere with his responsiveness to the present. In the *Lunch Poems* of Frank O'Hara, one of the best and most influential examples of the genre, where the present involves the vivid and constantly shifting street life of New York City, the poet, out for a casual stroll at lunch, is content to record his meandering impressions. His attitude is essentially aesthetic. The life around him is a shifting show, a show that includes him as a participant, stirring up within him a shifting flow of responses, and his one task is to be as open as he can to the various facts of his experience. In his inclusiveness O'Hara's speaker is a son of Whitman, but the facts he includes are not like Whitman's, limitless and holy. They are relentlessly commonplace, however graceful or comic or fresh, and the poems do not suggest that they can be changed more to our liking. How troubled we should feel by this essentially passive role for the poet, this denial of transforming power, is an issue that O'Hara himself addresses in one of his best-known poems, "The Day Lady Died":

It is 12:20 in New York a Friday
three days after Bastille day, yes
it is 1959 and I go get a shoeshine
because I will get off the 4:19 in Easthampton
at 7:15 and then go straight to dinner
and I don't know the people who will feed me

I walk up the muggy street beginning to sun
and have a hamburger and a malted and buy
an ugly NEW WORLD WRITING to see what the poets
in Ghana are doing these days
I go on to the bank
and Miss Stillwagon (first name Linda I once heard)
doesn't even look up my balance for once in her life
and in the GOLDEN GRIFFIN I get a little Verlaine
for Patsy with drawings by Bonnard although I do
think of Hesiod, trans. Richmond Lattimore or
Brendan Behan's new play or *Le Balcon* or *Les Nègres*
of Genet, but I don't, I stick with Verlaine
after practically going to sleep with quandariness

and for Mike I just stroll into the PARK LANE
Liquor Store and ask for a bottle of Strega and
then I go back where I came from to 6th Avenue
and the tobacconist in the Ziegfeld Theatre and
casually ask for a carton of Gauloises and a carton
of Picayunes, and a NEW YORK POST with her face on it

and I am sweating a lot by now and thinking of
leaning on the john door in the 5 SPOT
while she whispered a song along the keyboard
to Mal Waldron and everyone and I stopped
     breathing[7]

As an elegy for Billie Holiday, the poem calls attention to itself because only the last four lines are concerned with the speaker's response to the singer's death. The first twenty-five lines describe a casual afternoon of eating, banking, and buying presents for friends, emphatically unportentous activities that the poet seems to be enjoying. But the last four lines break the casual and comic mood. What might be ordinary sweating on a muggy day merges into the sweat of shock, and the speaker is pulled by his recollection out of the casual flow of the present into a state of breathless stillness that is produced by Holiday's singing. Holiday's death, then, makes an ordinary day, "three days after Bastille day," a momentous one, just as her art has made past occasions momentous. What makes the poem self-referential is the contrast it draws between Holiday's art, which resists the flow of ordinary life, and the speaker's listing of events, which seems to give the flow predominance. The difference is underscored by the powerful effects of Holiday's singing on her audience. For a moment her listeners become one, and this community, which includes the poet, makes the poet's efforts during the day to find connections seem pathetically inadequate. He has to make do with a dinner whose providers are unknown to him, with the trust of his bank teller, with the community of fellow writers met in an anthology. And though his careful gift-buying suggests that he cares about the particular tastes of his friends, he gives no indication that these individual friendships, important as they may be to him, are part of some larger whole. The poem, then, is built on contrasts that diminish the speaker's mode of life, though it is plotted so that the recollection of Holiday's power, reserved until the end, serves to break the tone of haphazard reporting, lifting the poet and his less powerful art out of the ordinary realm of surfaces.

A poet who turns from passive models of inclusiveness to active ones, who believes that impressions that reflect the moment need to be augmented by desires and possibilities that challenge the moment, has to be careful to avoid the kind of stridency and intolerance for which O'Hara's poetry serves as an antidote. Even if one is not tempted to system-building or the brooding nostalgia for the coherence of a lost culture, a critical stance runs the risk of imposing a theme on the world in a manner that is exclusive, that shrinks the world somewhat to make it comprehensible. To remain open we may have to learn to create speakers who resist from a position of uncertainty rather than counter a benighted certainty with an enlightened one. We can take as our model here Melville's Ishmael in *Moby Dick,* a quester who is willing to rest in doubt, as opposed to Ahab, who purchases his power of resistance at the cost of excluding all that does not support his single vision. Resisting Ahab's aggressive movement toward one goal, we may have to become, with Ishmael, masters of digression. The need for openness is especially clear when we recognize that the poetry of resistance will inevitably have a political dimension. To imagine alternatives to the life of the moment involves a critique of the existing conduct of public life, and the poet has to avoid thinking of his speaker as a spokesperson for any particular program or party. To be inclusive he has to create the voice of an explorer, not an expounder, an explorer who knows he must create his audience rather than presume one to be ready and waiting.

If the writer can achieve an individual voice that is open and critical, that can give the largest stage to private subjects and private resonance to public issues, his poem will produce an exhilaration that more modest poems cannot easily achieve, the pleasure of contact with a personality not intimidated by the world around it. In American poetry Whitman's expansive bard is a model for this kind of authority, a man at home everywhere, whose "elbows rest in sea gaps," whose "palms cover continents." Though American poets today may feel less at home on the planet, it isn't hard to think of several whose work often expresses large social and political concerns. But in my own gesture toward inclusiveness I want to choose an example from contemporary Eastern Europe, whose literature is now an inspiration to many American writers. Living until recently under oppressive governments, their writers have been impelled to focus much of their energies on political issues. Oppression, of course, is no guarantee of good poetry. It offers, in fact, the temptation of a rhetorical pose that makes good poetry impossible, the temptation toward the melodrama that casts political life as a struggle between powerless virtue and empowered evil. One of the remarkable things about the best of these poets is how they have worked to avoid this posture, how they have created speakers who try to take responsibility for as much as they can, to be not merely witnesses but participants, a part of the world they present, a part of the problem and a part of the cure, and how they test their imagination by constructing liberating alternatives to the present, rebuilding lost cities or imagining futures that challenge and complete the moment rather than merely reflect it. Consider this poem by the Polish poet Adam Zagajewski:

The Generation

TO THE MEMORY OF HELMUT KAJZAR

We walked very slowly down the concrete
slabs near the Olympic Stadium
in Berlin, where the black star
of Jesse Owens had flamed in that prehistoric
time, and the German air
had screamed. I wanted to laugh,
I couldn't believe you could walk
so slowly in the place he had run so fast;
to walk in one direction, but to look

in another, like the figures in Egyptian
reliefs. And yet we were walking that
way, bound with the light string
of friendship.
Two kinds of deaths circle about us.
One puts our whole group to sleep,
takes all of us, the whole herd.
Later it makes long speeches to substantiate
the sentence. The other one is wild, illiterate,
it catches us alone, strayed,
we animals, we bodies, we the pain,
we careless and uneducated.
We worship both of them in two religions
broken by schism. That scar
divided us sometimes when I had
forgotten: we have two deaths,
and one life.
Don't look back when you hear
my whisper. In the huge crowd of Greeks,
Egyptians, and Jews, in that fertile
generation turned to ashes, you walk straight
ahead, as then, unhurried,
alone.
The walls are not tight, windows open
at night to the rain, to the songs of stars
muffled by distance. But
every moment lasts eternally, becomes
a point, a haven, an envelope of emotion.
Every thought is a light coin which
rolls, in its shy secretive
being, into a song, into a painting. Every joy,

even the nonexistent one, leaves a transparent trace. Frost
kisses the pane because it can't get into the room.
This is how a new country arises,
built by us as if by mere chance,
constructed for the future, going down, in tunnels,
the bright shadow of the first country, an unfinished
house.[8]

The poem gives public resonance to a friendship by placing it in increasingly wider historical contexts. These contexts threaten the friendship as well as enlarge it because they suggest that the friends are shaped in part by historical forces they can't control, forces that bear on each of them differently. As Poles, both are drawn to the Olympic Stadium in Berlin as a shrine to the defeat of the Nazi theories of German superiority. But the poet is distant enough from the past to find some comedy in his friend's total absorption. Their different attitudes relate to differences between Jewish and Christian history. The "scar" of schism divides the two when the poet forgets that they experience the meaning of death differently, the Jew as a part of his communal history, the Christian as a private event:

That scar
divided us sometimes when I had
forgotten: we have two deaths,
and one life.

If the poem had ended here it would simply have given historical amplification to the limitations imposed on friendship. But at this point the speaker makes a bold leap. He tries to establish a posthumous relation with Kajzar that helps assert the power of the individual to resist contingency. Addressing Kajzar in the present tense, he encourages his friend to function as a model of affirmation of future possibilities. Because the dead Kajzar is in fact no longer in control of his life's meaning, we have to see the poet's exhortation to his friend as an exhortation to himself to resist the temptation to see the forces of history as beyond human control. Unlike Jesse Owens, Kajzar needs help to become a hero, and the poet tries to provide it by a series of bold generalizations that insist on human freedom:

> The walls are not tight, windows open
> at night to the rain, to the songs of stars
> muffled by distance. But
> every moment lasts eternally, becomes
> a point, a haven, an envelope of emotion.

These lines, and the string of assertions that follows them, are risky because they are not grounded on any facts we can point to in the poem. But their strain is perhaps deliberate. The speaker is trying to outline the creed of a new gospel, speaking, as a kind of oracle, shadowy pronouncements about a "new country" that is as yet unembodied, that is always prospective. All that supports it in the poem is the speaker's feelings for his friend, and this seems enough of a platform for the speaker's imagination to build its vision.

In moving from a rueful acceptance of limits to faith in the possibility of a "new country," Zagajewski's poem may be read as a challenge to those of us in America who have accepted too casually the notion that the central fact of modern political life is the powerlessness of the individual. If this notion can be resisted in Eastern Europe, surely it can be resisted here where the failures of our leaders reflect the failed insight of the people who elected them. America has always existed as two countries, the unembodied ideal that casts its "bright shadow," and the embodied fact. The painful discrepancy between the two may tempt us at times to narrow the range of our identifications so that the country's failure may not be felt as our own. But the virtues we seek in a voice of authority should work against this narrowing. They all involve the will to resist withdrawal from the world.

When we ask this of speakers who are passionate, we ask that they commit themselves to the importance of their subject rather than protect themselves from failure or foolishness by not taking themselves or their subject seriously. When we ask that they be discriminating, we ask that they reach their conclusions in dialogue with others (or with themselves conceived as an other) rather than in some unchallenged, self-admiring solitude. When we ask them to be inclusive, we ask them to consider all things within their range of interests, to find nothing for which they are not willing to assume at least some responsibility. The voice of authority is, finally, communal, not speaking for a community but directed toward the making of communities, beginning with the community of speaker and reader. It may be more difficult now for us to reach our audience than it was in traditional cultures in which poetry was able to confine itself to traditional materials. But a poet like Homer is still read because he did not define his audience too narrowly, and we can't be sure now to what extent Homer spoke for his culture and to what extent he helped create his culture by using the old stories in a new way. For all we know, Homer had as much work to do in making his community of readers as Odysseus had in reestablishing his home after an absence of twenty years. We should remember that the first time the *Odyssey* is told occurs near the end of the epic when Odysseus and Penelope, on their first night together again, tell each other all that happened during their separation. Stories are all they have to bridge the gap, and all that makes the stories effective is the willingness of the listener to believe. We can't expect such devoted listeners, but we can hope to win a hearing if our speakers make the effort to reach out.

CHAPTER TWO

Point of View

⚜

ALTHOUGH THE VIRTUES that I ascribe in the first chapter to every speaker of a poem all involve an engagement with the audience, they also allow for a range of possibilities with regard to the distance the speaker chooses to stand from his subject. When a speaker's passion is far more obvious than his discrimination and inclusiveness, and little space is allowed for reflection and expansion, we move toward unmediated engagement. When the situation is reversed, we move toward a poem of impersonal reflection. No poems are purely one mode or the other; but even in poems that avoid these extremes, the choice of distance, which is in essence a choice of which of the speaker's virtues are to be emphasized, is one of the most crucial in defining a particular personality.

The most obvious technical device for controlling the speaker's distance is choice of grammatical person—first person, second, and third, singular and plural. These options are somewhat qualified by our sense that even in the third person the poet's voice, not usually mediated by narrative, is likely to feel closer to us than the voice of a narrator in fiction, addressing us more directly and required to win at once our complete confidence that she or he is reliable. The very fact that we use the term "poet" for the maker of the poem as well as the speaker is a sign of the greater presence we demand from a poetic voice than we demand from the narrator of a work of fiction. However different the speaker may be from the writer, we assume that the writer has chosen a voice he finds congenial, through which he can explore his deepest concerns. But even with this restriction in stepping back from their subjects, poets still have significant freedom with regard to the point of view of particular poems, and most poets make use of this freedom in choosing a variety of grammatical persons even though they may favor one mode over the others. What I want to show in this chapter is that this technical choice is a function of the virtues that the writer wants the speaker to exemplify.

In American poetry the use of variety of persons is vividly illustrated by the practice of our great nineteenth-century originals, Whitman and Dickinson. We may think of Whitman in his catalogs as an omniscient demigod who can list everything that America contains, but he is also a particular "I" with a fully developed personality, celebrating his likes and dislikes, and this "I" is a master at addressing "you," the reader whom he wants to enlighten, encourage, and inspire. Similarly we may think of Dickinson as the writer of private, wrenching, first-person lyrics, but she is also clearly the master of impersonal statement, the maker of categorical pronouncements on the human condition. Becoming familiar with a poet is in part a process of becoming familiar with a range of rhetorical stances. Dickinson is an especially interesting writer in this regard because her themes are few. The variety in her work results almost entirely from variety in approach, which is in good part a function of the degree of distance she chooses to take toward her material. For this reason I want to use her poems as a reference point here, beginning in each mode with her example before reaching out to suggest how other writers use point of view to create speakers that engage and challenge.

The most obvious rule of thumb in the handling of distance is that a detached speaker is likely to be best presented in the third person and an engaged speaker in the first person. But this rule leaves unanswered the more basic question of which perspective, detachment or engagement, allows the more fruitful approach to the particular material that the poet chooses to develop. Finding the answer to this question may involve the writer in a long process of trial and error. In Dickinson's work, this issue is perhaps raised most clearly by the poems she chooses to write in an impersonal voice, for often their subject matter, intense pain or joy, would seem to call for first-person immediacy. Coming upon these poems for the first time, one is likely to ask why the poet has chosen to handle her material at so great a remove. Consider the eight-line poem "The Heart asks Pleasure—first":

> The Heart asks Pleasure—first—
> And then—Excuse from Pain—
> And then—those little Anodynes
> That deaden suffering—
>
> And then—to go to sleep—
> And then—if it should be
> The will of its Inquisitor
> The privilege to die— [1]

In presenting life as a sequence of diminishing expectations from hope to despair, the poem seems to be presented in just the person least likely to be convincing. What we might accept as a first-person account of the speaker's own experience risks sounding strained and hyperbolic when extended to everyone by impersonal assertion. And yet, despite our logical objections to the poem's gloomy view of life, the poem somehow manages to be rhetorically convincing. If we don't agree with its generalizations, we are at least convinced that the speaker is making assertions not from a provincial limitation of experience or from a momentary bleakness of mood but from a careful consideration that has resulted in a tone of quiet conviction. This effect is gained in part by the discrimination of five separate attitudes toward life, which suggests a speaker whose generalizing does not prevent her from making important distinctions. And this judiciousness is supported by the remarkable concision of the poem, which allows the speaker to express these five stages of the heart in the brief scope of eight lines, a concision that seems to be the result of a long process of distillation. We may not want to believe the poem, but we are convinced that whoever is speaking deserves our attention and respect. We are challenged by the statement, forced to enter into dialogue with it, as we would not be challenged if the poem were written in the first person and we could regard it as the expression of one person's limited history:

> My Heart asks Pleasure—first—
> And then—Excuse from Pain—
> And then—those little Anodynes
> That deaden suffering—
>
> And then—to go to sleep—
> And then—if it should be
> The will of my Inquisitor
> The privilege to die—

The speaker here is making a statement that is far less likely to be disputed than the statement of Dickinson's speaker, but she purchases her credibility at the cost of our engagement because she does little to make us care about her problems. The general language that works well when used by an omniscient speaker describing the course of any life sounds curiously vague and evasive when applied to the speaker's own life. She seems to be trying to win our sympathy for her suffering without allowing us to judge on our own whether or not her gloom is justified. Clear-eyed observation is replaced by self-serving sentimentality. In saying less, the first-person version sounds immodest, while in the original, which makes far grander claims to insight, the speaker sounds decorous and restrained.

Our sense of the greater depth and strength of Dickinson's speaker is intensified to the extent that we feel, under the presence of "the heart," a "my heart" that has been transcended. Though we are not told how the speaker has arrived at her gloomy perspective about the human condition, we assume that personal experience plays at least some role. But in the boldness of her distilled summations she has chosen emphatically not to present herself as a victim, as the weak, broken beggar described at the end of the poem, who passively waits for death from a cruel tormentor. She is strong in her unflinching determination to name the limits of life. Against the inquisitor who takes away our freedom, she functions as the witness who asserts her freedom to anatomize the forces that the heart has to contend with. Because the speaker and sufferer are disjoined, the poem sounds much less despairing in tone than a literal paraphrase would seem to entail. Logically the speaker's heart is included in the poem's generalizations about the diminishment of human hope and power, but rhetorically we are made to feel that the speaker has reached a quiet vantage point far above the spot where the suffering heart slowly goes under.

The distance achieved by the speaker in Dickinson's poem gives a moral dimension to the third-person omniscient perspective. Distance in this context means moving beyond personal outrage to a dispassionate statement of truth, means boldly stating, without evasion, the dark truth about human limits. In contrast we can distinguish a third-person distance that is essentially aesthetic rather than moral, that associates impersonality with the ability to do justice to positive forces latent in the world, to be in touch with the kind of beauty and energy that is hidden from those who would approach the world with their own subjective agenda. In such a poem the third person is usually objective rather than omniscient. William Carlos Williams probably comes first to mind in this regard, whose stated policy of replacing "I am" with "there is" is done in the service of embodying a greater openness to the world. Often this very replacement is one of the subjects of the poem, as it seems to be in his famous description of a red wheelbarrow:

> so much depends
> upon
>
> a red wheel
> barrow
>
> glazed with rain
> water
>
> beside the white
> chickens.[2]

This poem is built on a series of small surprises in which the speaker raises our expectations about the focus of the poem and then suddenly subverts them. In the first stanza he boldly announces a grand and general topic, nothing less than the existence of some independent kind of being on which "so much depends," but that entity of crucial importance, we find in the anticlimactic second stanza, is only a homely and specific red wheelbarrow. We are left with a paradox that we assume the poet will explain in the rest of the poem, but instead of an explanation we are given only more details about the wheelbarrow that emphasize its particularity. The apparently omniscient speaker of the first two stanzas now adopts an objective stance, leaving us to figure out the discrepancy for ourselves. This shift is particularly surprising if we approach the poem with expectations raised by traditional poems that make claims for the importance of apparently insignificant objects. We expect a set of personal associations that would embed the wheelbarrow in the speaker's life or in the lives of his relations, or at least in a third-person human drama, associations that would make the object into an emotional symbol like the "fly" in Emily Dickinson's "I heard a Fly buzz—when I died" or like the sheepfold in Wordsworth's "Michael." Instead, the objective second half suggests that value does not come from the symbolic overtones the poet imparts to an object but from our openness to literal context, though this context is accidental (beaded with raindrops and beside white chickens) and momentary (lasting only until the drops evaporate and the chickens move). The speaker's antisymbolist, antitranscendent way of seeing is embodied for us as well in the short and broken lines of the poem, which give emphasis to seemingly unimportant parts of speech like prepositions and adjectives, as well as to nouns and verbs, and so suggest that in reading the poem, just as in understanding the scene described, every element has to be given its importance as part of the whole.

The rhetorical risk run with the omniscient voice of moral generalization is that the reader will either judge the statement as too obvious or too unqualified. In the poem of aesthetic distance, the risk is that the objectively rendered scene will seem mere neutral description, without a clear point of view. Williams is willing to run such a risk in order to root his poems in the concrete world, but he often anticipates and avoids the risk by enacting within his poems a shift from neutrality to engagement that offers a minimalist embodiment of imaginative activity. This method is used to telling effect in *Pictures from Brueghel,* where the implications of Brueghel's objective paintings are presented as available to the reader willing to look with care and sympathy. Here is "Self-Portrait":

In a red winter hat blue
eyes smiling
just the head and shoulders

crowded on the canvas
arms folded one
big ear the right showing
the face slightly tilted
a heavy wool coat
with broad buttons

gathered at the neck reveals
a bulbous nose
but the eyes red-rimmed
from over-use he must have
driven them hard
but the delicate wrists

show him to have been a
man unused to
manual labor unshaved his
blond beard half trimmed
no time for any-
thing but his painting.[3]

The first eleven lines give us in quick strokes an inventory of some basic images of the painting, but they don't give us a perspective. The red hat and wool coat with broad buttons don't convey any mood, and the "smiling" blue eyes are not followed by any other features that might indicate character, just by the staccato, disconnected details of folded arms, big ear, and bulbous nose. With line 9, however, the word "but" clearly introduces a countermovement. Now the details come with commentary that involves a movement from the outer to the inner man. The poet is still an objective observer, but now his objectivity is informed by a sympathetic imagination that can see prosy facts like red-rimmed eyes, thin wrists, and unkempt beard as expressive of the painter's engagement with his art. The crucial last word of the poem implies an emphatic shift of subject from the visible painting before us to the vocation of painting, which is present only to a viewer who is willing to fill in a world that is only suggested. But the act of filling in that the speaker performs here is not done by reading into the painting, the poem implies, only by reading out. The imagination supplies an enlightened identification with the subject rather than imposing upon it the viewer's private impressions.

The great attraction of the third-person poem is that it gives the reader the sense of transcending the narrowness of a subjective point of view, that it expresses the possibility of presenting the world without the mediation of a particular personality with its needs and expectations. The drawback is that it can't do full justice to the experience we have of our individual selves as the center of our consciousness and the object of our deepest concern. If Emily Dickinson had written only third-person poems with omniscient voices, she would still be a great poet, but we would not have the voice we are likely to think of first in calling to mind her poetry, that of the individual suffering self trying to make sense of a dispensation that seems bent on denying her deepest wishes. Such first-person poems, to be sure, have their own rhetorical liabilities, most obviously the danger of presenting a speaker who sounds too self-absorbed to be engaging, whose inner life seems to have no windows and doors for the reader to enter. Dickinson would seem a likely candidate for this constriction because her first-person poems do not tend to focus on her relations with others, at least do not do so in a way that allows those others any central place. They turn inward, providing a space for her speakers to examine the feelings produced by her encounters. What saves the speaker of such a poem from sounding self-imprisoned is the poet's skill in making a place within a subjective perspective for a third-person distance. In the case of Dickinson, her voices achieve their distinctive power in good part because they don't purchase their intensity at the cost of breadth, even when the poems suggest the uniqueness rather than the typicality of the speaker's experience.

To see the role of distance in the shaping of Dickinson's first-person voice, it might be useful to look at another poem about the loss of faith, "I shall know why—when Time is over":

> I shall know why—when Time is over—
> And I have ceased to wonder why—
> Christ will explain each separate anguish
> In the fair schoolroom of the sky—
>
> He will tell me what "Peter" promised—
> And I—for wonder at his woe—
> I shall forget the drop of Anguish
> That scalds me now—that scalds me now!

The poem ends with a direct statement of the speaker's suffering, but this directness is given special weight by being placed at the end of the speaker's attempts to distance herself from her suffering through religious consolation. In heaven her present suffering will be explained as meaningful in the context of some encompassing purpose now hidden from her and will be made to feel small in the context of Christ's suffering for mankind. This effort to stand back from her pain and place it in a larger context is made simultaneously with a second act of distancing that casts doubt on the efficacy of the consolation even as it's being offered. The figure of heaven as a schoolroom suggests that in order to accept the religious explanations one has to enter into a second childhood, to summon up the kind of unquestioning faith that the speaker is no longer able to summon. And if answers come, they do so only when she "has ceased to wonder why," when she no longer wants them or needs them. Even if Christ speaks to her in heaven about the church Peter establishes, his words will be less important than his silent woe in helping her take her mind off her own troubles. And the thought of that fellowship still does nothing to answer the immediate problem of suffering on earth. In the emphatic repetition of the last line, the dream of consolation is punctured by the actual cry of pain, a pain the speaker cannot transcend or escape. And yet the effort has in the meantime significantly enlarged the speaker's perspective and in doing so has won the reader's assent. We cannot dismiss the "scalding" as the hyperbole of someone who enjoys dramatizing her suffering. Here is a speaker who would like to believe that her suffering is limited in time and scope, and is painfully disappointed.

The difference between what the speaker says overtly about religious faith and what is in fact implied may make us want to experiment here with the further act of distancing that occurs when we shift the "I" of the poem to a "they." What would be lost or gained if the poem were called "The Believers" and the poet did not include herself among the faithful?

They shall know why—when Time is over—
And they have ceased to wonder why—
Christ will explain each separate anguish
In the fair schoolroom of the sky—

He will tell them what "Peter" promised—
And they—for wonder at his woe—
They shall forget the drop of Anguish
That scalds them now—that scalds them now!

A defender of this poem might argue that it is superior to the first-person version in the same way that the third-person version of "The Heart asks Pleasure—first" is superior to the first-person rewrite. Instead of private complaint, based on the speaker's sense that the heavenly consolations have failed her, it expresses a compassion with others, a broad understanding that such consolations have failed all believers. But the differences between the third-person versions are telling. In "The Heart asks Pleasure—first," the speaker is indirectly implicated in the workings of "the heart," but in "They Shall Know Why" the speaker is more enlightened than the people she is describing. She sees the truth about heavenly promises while the believers remain deluded. As a result the speaker sounds patronizing even if the reader is convinced her compassion is genuine. The reference of the poem is enlarged but the theme is diminished because the illusion described here is presented as avoidable by the knowing. In Dickinson's poem, which places the conflict between innocence and experience within the mind of the speaker, the issue is made to seem a permanent condition of spiritual consciousness. The personal poem turns out, paradoxically, to be more universal, more inclusive, than the poem that literally includes more people as its subject. It invites both believer and nonbeliever to identify with the speaker's inner drama.

The contrasts between the third-person version of "I Shall Know Why" and the version Dickinson actually wrote make clear that the ironies of Dickinson's speaker do not in any way diminish the significance of her plight. She finds religious promises wanting, but she considers her suffering just as deserving of solace as the suffering of those who have turned to God in their trials. And if in a conventional heaven her anguish would appear as a "drop" compared to Christ's, on earth it does not feel diminished by the comparison. Indeed, through the Biblical allusions, the speaker of the poem attains a kind of heroic status as sufferer, and the ironic tone is used not to under-

mine that status but to suggest that it is partly constituted by a rejection of illusion. This mythologizing of the individual self, which justifies our thinking of Dickinson as a Romantic poet, is one of her great
poetic achievements, an achievement especially hard to carry off in
the first person, where the risk of sounding self-aggrandizing is at its
greatest. Against a first-person Romantic need she opposes a disillu-
sioned third-person shrewdness about the absurdity of that need, creating a tense, dynamic balance.

Most poems in the first person avoid solipsism not only by incor-
porating some self-critical distance but by expanding the subject matter of the poem beyond the self, as is the case with the first-person
poems we looked at in the first chapter. The voices of Yeats, O'Hara,
and Zagajewski are obviously, in the examples discussed, turned outward, engaged with others in their immediate environment or with
the world in general. The post-Romantic poets who have sometimes
been charged with solipsism are those often called "confessional,"
and my somewhat critical reading of Lowell's poem "Alfred Corning
Clark" suggests that his elegy is not outward-turning enough, given
its stated intention. But the best of their work avoids the problem even
when it presents a speaker who is solitary and self-absorbed. As my
test case I want to look at a poem by Sylvia Plath, whose speaker at
times reminds one of Dickinson's in her radical estrangement from
the world. Here is "Last Words":

> I do not want a plain box, I want a sarcophagus
> With tigery stripes, and a face on it
> Round as the moon, to stare up.
> I want to be looking at them when they come
> Picking among the dumb minerals, the roots.
> I see them already—the pale, star-distance faces.
> Now they are nothing, they are not even babies.
> I imagine them without fathers or mothers, like the first gods.

They will wonder if I was important.
I should sugar and preserve my days like fruit!
My mirror is clouding over—
A few more breaths, and it will reflect nothing at all.
The flowers and faces whiten to a sheet.

I do not trust the spirit. It escapes like steam
In dreams, through mouth-hole or eye-hole. I can't stop it.
One day it won't come back. Things aren't like that.
They stay, their little particular lusters
Warmed by much handling. They almost purr.
When the soles of my feet grow cold,
The blue eye of my turquoise will comfort me.
Let me have my copper cooking pots, let my rouge pots
Bloom about me like night flowers, with a good smell.
They will roll me up in bandages, they will store my heart
Under my feet in a neat parcel.
I shall hardly know myself. It will be dark,
And the shine of these small things sweeter than the face of Ishtar.[4]

It would be hard to think of a more solitary speaker than the one we are given here, uttering her "last words" only to herself, planning a funeral that does not prompt her to imagine any mourners. The people she places at the grave arrive far in the future, strangers with "star-distance faces" who are not yet born, and she can supply them with no clear reason to be digging up her remains beyond that of impersonal archaeology. They may wonder whether she "was important," but she does not believe they will move beyond this vague curiosity about status to learn who she actually might have been, and they have no means to do so even if they should want to. In such a lonely situation one may suppose that the speaker would be led to turn from the disappointing world to some transcendent realm, but in fact she "do[es] not trust the spirit" to offer any lasting companionship, and so she must make do simply with the companionship of the few things she is buried with, her cooking pots and rouge pots. What gives the poem its dramatic tension is that the speaker's tone is free from any of the bitterness and complaint one might be led to expect. Instead, one finds a voice of impressive self-assurance. The speaker views her end as a chance to express at least some of her deepest wishes. Her opening wish for "a sarcophagus with tigery stripes," as opposed to a plain box, suggests she sees death in theatrical terms. Her play has no audience but herself, it's true, but this audience seems to suffice. And as she becomes more solitary her grand role becomes more obvious. Her emphatic statements of preference are taken from the script of an ancient queen. She is to play the part of a Cleopatra who speaks in commands to her invisible serving women about how her "things" are to be disposed in the grave with her mummified remains. To the vulgar observer such an end is anything but regal, but to the speaker bent on doing the best with the part she has been given or has chosen, her wish to find the "small things sweeter than the face of Ishtar" will be a heroic achievement. Ishtar, the great fertility goddess who descended into the underworld in search of her lover, need not come for the poet, who doesn't expect deliverance and doesn't pine for it. Dickinson's speaker in "I shall know why" achieves a heroism of grand demands by a refusal to take disappointment meekly. Plath's speaker achieves a heroism of grand gesture by a performance before an audience of one on a stage that she recognizes to be no bigger than the grave.

Turning first-person isolation into a badge of insight about the human condition, as Dickinson and Plath do, gives their speakers a peculiar power that continues to exert its influence on poets writing today, though most contemporary poets also make an effort to use other voices that are deliberately turned outward. The most obvious register of that intention involves the use, within the first-person poem, of the second person and first-person plural. The "I" of such a poem addresses the reader directly as a "you," and "I" and "you" together form a "we" who share certain experiences and perspectives. In American poetry the great exemplar of this strategy is Dickinson's grand antinomy, Whitman, who confidently asserts his ability to divine and encourage the reader's deepest aspirations:

> I celebrate myself, and sing myself,
> And what I assume you shall assume,
> For every atom belonging to me as good belongs to you.

So Whitman's Walt opens "Song of Myself," and by the end of the poem he has enacted the challenge implicit in his assertion of comradeship by pointing his listeners to the road that is open to those who are as confident and adventurous as he is, who have earned the right to depend on his human example and support:

> Failing to fetch me at first keep encouraged,
> Missing me one place search another,
> I stop somewhere waiting for you.

Whitman's confidence that his speaker can connect with everyone comes in part from his belief that the self is a compendium of all the selves called into consciousness by ordinary experience in the world, experience that in our democratic America should be available to all and provide for continual growth as long as the borders of the self are kept open. For Dickinson's embattled poet, on the other hand, who sees the self as defined in good part by its opposition to the world around it, any easy presumption of comradeship is a form of self-deception. So if we tried to change "I shall know why" to "We shall know why," the falseness of the willed sociability would be immediately evident:

We shall know why—when Time is over—
And we have ceased to wonder why—
Christ will explain each separate anguish
In the fair schoolroom of the sky.

He will tell us what "Peter" promised—
And we—for wonder at his woe—
We shall forget the drop of Anguish
That scalds us now—that scalds us now!

This "we" is offensive because it presumes a shared assumption that
the reader may be unwilling to grant. The reader may not feel disappointed by life, and if disappointed may have never harbored the religious hopes that have led the speaker to disappointment. And if he
believed such promises, he may still take comfort in them. In the first-
person singular we are free to engage ourselves as deeply as we choose
with the script that the speaker offers, but the plural allows no alternatives to total consent. We feel we are being bullied, and so refuse to
become engaged in what is being said. In this regard, it is significant
that of the handful of Dickinson's poems that address the reader directly, the best-known presents the "I" and the "you" as a single pair
in opposition to a dominant "they":

I'm Nobody! Who are you?
Are you—Nobody—Too?
Then there's a pair of us?
Don't tell! they'd advertise—you know!

How dreary—to be—Somebody!
How public—like a Frog—
To tell one's name—the livelong June—
To an admiring Bog!

The speaker and the "you" here are "nobodies," people without important social place, who share a sense of superiority to the "somebodies" who find themselves affirmed only by constant public acclaim. Poet and reader form a community based not on mutual need but on their freedom from the need for recognition, a community of self-delighting individuals.

For the poet who wants to follow Whitman's lead and address the reader directly, Dickinson's example offers a cautionary suspicion that using "we" makes us liable to presuming on a connection that does not exist. Whitman's speaker manages to pull off his presumption by his tone of genuine interest in his reader's welfare, by a comic genius that is aware of his own outlandish claims to intimacy, and by a poetic invention so full of brio that it convinces us we are lucky to have inspired the poet's interest. But most poets are more cautious in claiming a connection with the reader, and most readers are resistant to the presumption of familiarity, a resistance that Eliot's Prufrock arouses at the beginning of his "Love Song":

> Let us go then, you and I,
> When the evening is spread out against the sky
> Like a patient etherised upon a table.

We do not wish to go with such a guide on such a journey. We resist the impertinence implied by his assuming we need to learn about what he has to show us; but by the end of the poem we are forced to acknowledge his difficulties are ours, that the "you" and "I" can rightly be encompassed by a "we":

> We have lingered in the chambers of the sea
> By sea-girls wreathed with seaweed red and brown
> Till human voices wake us, and we drown.

We may wish to maintain an Emersonian faith in the private self, but the pronoun here suggests that even in our fantasies our individuality has been undermined by the forces of the modern world.

But the use of "we" in a poem is not always either presumptuous or a confession of a want of moral autonomy. If the poet intends to regard any trait or condition as general to human nature, and wants to view the subject from within rather than from without, the first-person plural is likely to be the best choice. So "we" seems inevitable in this poem by Lisel Mueller called "Things":

What happened is, we grew lonely
living among the things,
so we gave the clock a face,
the chair a back,
the table four stout legs
which will never suffer fatigue.

We fitted our shoes with tongues
as smooth as our own
and hung tongues inside bells
so we could listen
to their emotional language,

and because we loved graceful profiles
the pitcher received a lip,
the bottle a long, slender neck.

Even what was beyond us
was recast in our image;
we gave the country a heart,
the storm an eye,
the cave a mouth
so we could pass into safety.[5]

Here "we" seems right partly because the speaker does not presume any personal connection between her and a particular you. The "we" does not so much refer to the reader in particular but to the whole human race. This more general "we" takes some of the pressure off the reader to give his immediate approval or disapproval to the speaker's statements. And this strategy is supported by the modesty of the particular aspect of human nature that is here asserted to be shared by everyone. Our languages personify common things about us not because we wish to dominate the world with an imperial epistemology but because "we grew lonely," because of a basic human need to live in a world that feels familiar, not remote and impersonal. And we begin not with the far away but with the things that come from our own hands, as if in our loneliness we are frail enough to believe that even those items we can most rightly call ours are in some danger of being estranged from us. Each of the first three stanzas raises the claim of connection to a higher intimacy, from the servant-like chair and stout-legged table, to the fellowship of the smooth-tongued shoe and articulate bells with their "emotional language," to the ideal of human beauty embodied in the lipped pitcher and slender-necked bottle. When the "we" finally turns to personifying the natural world "beyond us," the reader is prepared to see it not as an egotistical assertion of human primacy but as the final expression of our need to make the world less menacing, so that vast spaces, storms, and caves can be felt as offering some kind of shelter, can let us "pass into [the] safety" that we would like to expect of a place we consider home. Our language is the record of our needs, and our needs are not weaknesses to be transcended but simply to be recognized and accepted openly as we come to clarity about who we are.

The use of the first-person plural in Mueller's poem might suggest that the speaker is likely to avoid claiming too much when the "we" includes more than the speaker and the reader, but generalizations are difficult here because each "we" is different from every other. Consider the control of point of view in Dickinson's "There's a certain Slant of light," which presents us with a far more specific context than does Mueller's "Things":

There's a certain Slant of light,
Winter Afternoons—
That oppresses, like the Heft
Of Cathedral Tunes—

Heavenly Hurt, it gives us—
We can find no scar,
But internal difference,
Where the Meanings, are—

None may teach it—Any—
'Tis the Seal Despair—
An imperial affliction
Sent us of the Air—

When it comes, the Landscape listens—
Shadows—hold their breath—
When it goes, 'tis like the Distance
On the look of Death—

Both the concreteness of the occasion—the noticing of a particular light on a particular kind of day—and the subjective focus—the impression that the light makes on the viewer—might lead one to expect a poem in the first-person singular. We are not presented here, after all, with a group experience, but with what seems to be the speaker's private feelings. But if we try to shift the poem into the singular, we can see at once that its meaning gets compromised. "Heavenly hurt it gives me" might suggest that the speaker's response to the light is based on personal and self-aggrandizing associations, the result of her own peculiar history, while the "us" suggests what the poem in fact bears out, that the speaker views the light as carrying the same meaning for everyone, that it brings to consciousness what it means to be a human being, a creature aware of its own mortality. The light that leaves the landscape under a pall of death reminds us all that we will die. And the hurt it gives us is "heavenly" because our knowledge of our own imminent death makes us spiritual creatures, creatures who comprehend their limits and so are impelled to ask questions about the meaning of their lives. To help establish the generality of reference in the poem, the speaker withholds the personal pronoun in the first stanza. Had she asserted, "We see a certain slant of light," she might have appeared to be placing at issue the objectivity of the experience. "There's a certain slant of light" suggests that everyone responds to the light, as to cathedral music, in a similar way. By the time the first-person plural appears, as the direct object in a sentence in which light is the subject, the freedom of the "us" seems limited to understanding a response that we cannot alter. At the end of the poem, where the landscape is presented as a participant in the action, the "we" again disappears, and the landscape seems not so much to mirror the speaker's projections as to provide our shared inner response with an objective corroboration. All things, even shadows, feel what we feel. The careful control of distance here, which gives to subjective experience a communal and objective weight, makes the poem peculiarly effective.

But when Dickinson wants to engage her reader more directly than the first or third person will allow, she usually turns not to the communal "we" but to a special form of the second person in which the speaker remains aloof, the "you" being addressed by the speaker in ways that insist on the distance between them. Sometimes the address consists of direct imperatives, sometimes indirectly in the form of riddles that seem to be meant to puzzle the reader as much as illuminate. Consider "Some things that fly there be," which uses the term "riddle" to define its central statement:

> Some things that fly there be—
> Birds—Hours—the Bumblebee—
> Of these no Elegy.
>
> Some things that stay there be—
> Grief—Hills—Eternity—
> Nor this behooveth me.
>
> There are that resting, rise.
> Can I expound the skies?
> How still the Riddle lies!

This poem is partly in the third person, spoken by an omniscient poet who confidently divides the world up into three kinds of things, and partly in the first person, the words of someone who sees her task as particularly involved in exploring the mysterious "things" of the last stanza, the things that "resting, rise." But the presence of the reader is implied by the use of language that is deliberately paradoxical, that suggests the poet is trying not to communicate her thoughts directly so much as to test the reader's depth of understanding by offering a riddle only the enlightened will be able to decipher. We are left to find the answer ourselves and so prove that we are ready for the truth that lies concealed here, ready to do justice to those things that are both ephemeral and permanent, a doubleness that presumably defines the realm of the human that the speaker tells us it behooves her to dwell on. This kind of poem may be called oracular. It seems to come out of a tradition that relates the use of cryptic language to the testing of a would-be candidate for a spiritual revelation that frees him or her from the ordinary categories of thought. When Dickinson writes in this mode, her speaker is overtly a teacher, like Whitman's poet, though her mode of instruction is different from Whitman's. The

Walt of the *Leaves* is a familiar prophet, leading us by the arm to the top of the knoll where he points us to the open road before us and offers himself as an enlightened, model companion. The speaker of Dickinson's cryptic poems presents herself, on the other hand, as a sibyl, withholding and reserving her deepest truth for the few among the many who can prove themselves able to embrace the paradoxes of spiritual life.

The immediate influence on Dickinson in the use of an oracular style is Emerson, and like him she tends to use it most obviously in poems intended to suggest the reader's failure to appreciate deeply enough the limitless depths of the soul. It would be hard to think of a poem that would have pleased Emerson more in style and theme, had he been able to read it, than "The Brain—is wider than the Sky," which follows his poem "The Sphinx" in its use of challenging paradoxes:

> The Brain—is wider than the Sky—
> For—put them side by side—
> The one the other will contain
> With ease—and You—beside—
>
> The Brain is deeper than the sea—
> For—hold them—Blue to Blue—
> The one the other will absorb—
> As Sponges—Buckets—do—
>
> The Brain is just the weight of God—
> For—Heft them—Pound for Pound—
> And they will differ—if they do—
> As Syllable from Sound—

Even without the aside to the reader in line four, the presence of the reader is indicated here by a style that is meant to perplex, that employs a string of apparent absurdities to push the reader beyond ordinary categories of thought. Substituting the physiological term "brain" for "mind" only makes the comparisons seem more incomprehensible and so even more in need of a reading that will abandon a literal perspective for a figurative one. Yet the speaker does not seem to be detached from the world. In using the homeliest of terms to talk about the workings of the mind—sponges, buckets, weights, and syllables—and in wittily insisting on a literal juxtaposition of incommensurables, she suggests that someone sufficiently enlightened can find analogues in the material world to clarify the workings of the soul. But the truth of the analogies is left for the reader to discover on his own. And only the reader willing to accept being confused as a prerequisite for enlightenment is likely to be successful.

The model of Emerson and Dickinson has often inspired subsequent American poets to try their hands at using an oracular speaker who favors a confrontational use of the second person. We can find the voice at times in Pound's *Cantos,* or in Eliot's *Four Quartets,* or, more consistently and directly, in a poem like Frost's "Directive," whose speaker, directing us to "a town that is no more a town," tells us that he "only has at heart [our] getting lost." For a contemporary and more comic version of this mode, I want to close this chapter with Charles Simic's poem "Club Midnight":

> Are you the sole owner of a seedy nightclub?
>
> Are you its sole customer, sole bartender,
> Sole waiter prowling around the empty tables?
>
> Do you put on wee-hour girlie shows
> With dead stars of black-and-white films?
>
> Is your office upstairs over the neon lights,
> Or down deep in the dank rat cellar?

Are bearded Russian thinkers your silent partners?
Do you have a doorman by the name of Dostoyevsky?

Is Fu Manchu coming tonight?
Is Miss Emily Dickinson?

Do you happen to have an immortal soul?
Do you have a sneaky suspicion that you have none?

Is that why you throw a white pair of dice,
In the dark, long after the joint closes? [6]

Though the speaker here is addressing the reader, the questions he is asking seem, at first, too pointed and too odd to invite us in. No, we are not the owner of a seedy nightclub, is our immediate response. You've sent your questionnaire to the wrong person. But by the end of the second stanza it becomes clear that this nightclub is a metaphor for a particular kind of mental life, one that the speaker is suggesting may be relevant to each of his readers. Accepting the connection may be a somewhat humiliating process, for we have to admit to girlie-show fantasies and misty nostalgia for the screen stars of our youth; but by the end of the fourth stanza the speaker has presumed far enough to assume that the issue is not whether the links are true but whether our office is upstairs or down, whether we manage, in our somewhat shabby and squalid state, to keep our hopes up or have chosen to embrace the dark perspective of an underground man. Once we have reached this stage of recognition, the speaker is willing to enlarge the limits of our condition by adding characters to the solitude that suggest we have a more thoughtful side as well, one that reflects on the meaning of things, though we are given no assurance that this disposition is rooted more deeply than is its trivial partner. It's just as likely that "Fu Manchu" is dropping by as the earnest "Miss Emily Dickinson," just as likely that we don't have an immortal soul as that we do, and only the luck we may hope for in dream may provide us with one.

The force of this witty and challenging poem is in large part the result of the use of the interrogatory form of the second person. As declarative statement the speaker would sound too knowing, insistent, and moralistic. In Simic's version the speaker is asking us to try his questions on for size, and in the process seems to be mocking the generality of official questionnaires with an unofficial and specific alternative. And the attempt to try "I" or "he" here would leave us with speakers who would present other difficulties. A questioning first-person voice would leave us wondering why the speaker was playing the rhetorical game of asking himself questions he knew the answers to ("Am I the sole owner of a seedy nightclub?"), and a first-person direct statement would sound vain, as if the speaker were boasting about the densely paradoxical nature of his character ("I am the sole owner of a seedy nightclub"). In the third person, on the other hand, whether interrogatory or direct ("Is he the owner of a seedy night club?" or "He is the owner of a seedy nightclub"), we would be left wanting to know why this oddly defined person should be of interest to the speaker or to us. In the poem we have, in which the speaker is present simply as the poser of witty, challenging questions, we are drawn in, willing to acknowledge the truth of the description even as we protest that its metaphors are not the whole story.

Simic's mention of "Miss Emily Dickinson" takes us back, by way of contrast, to our starting point. Dickinson appears in his poem as representative of one distinct mood. In this chapter she appears as an example of a poet who uses a wide range of persons to embody a variety of virtues. The distance her characteristic speaker assumes shifts from poem to poem, as even the different tonality of her two riddle poems make clear, the direct challenge of "The Brain Is Wider Than the Sky" as opposed to the more private and tentative quality of "Some Things That Fly There Be." The shifting proportion of involvement and detachment we find in her work seems even more varied than the range of mood from faith to disillusionment, from joy to despair. No poet has a more distinctive voice than Dickinson, but this voice turns out to be made up of a mosaic of different local voices. Calm observer, needy petitioner, riddling oracle—each appears on the stage of the poem in many different guises, sometimes alone, sometimes in the presence of others, giving to similar themes a rich variety of implication.

What her speakers share is a strongly assertive, solitary individuality that at the same time remains aware of the world around her, if only as an option that for her is closed. For all their embattled privacies, their perspective turns out to be inclusive because they maintain enough distance to view their problems in a way that manages to invite identification, to relate them to the whole human condition. The reason we prefer her poems to the revisions offered here turns out to be fundamentally an ethical one. We like her speakers more. We prefer to be in their society because they seem at the same time wiser and more compassionate, far-seeing without indifference or superiority, involved without narrow self-absorption. The self here is not a prison house that the speaker is powerless to escape. It is full of ennobling projects, however thwarted or doomed they may be. But it is also transcended by acts of distancing, so that the reader, without being flattered, cajoled, or presumed upon, is eager to engage the poetry in fruitful dialogue.

CHAPTER THREE

Irony

BESIDES POINT OF VIEW, one of the most common devices for controlling a speaker's distance is irony, which sets up a discrepancy between the apparent meaning and the implied meaning. The trope is often used in the service of mockery, as when praise is offered for something unworthy, so it is often associated with satire, especially with traditional satire, which depends on a shared sense of appropriate and inappropriate behavior. To the extent that irony implies a privileged circle of those who understand artful indirection, as opposed to those who require everything to be plainly spelled out, the trope risks sounding condescending. And it comes as no surprise that Whitman, who insists that he speaks to everyone, and especially to men and women of common life, almost never uses irony, while Dickinson, who believes in an aristocracy of suffering, of enlightened privation, makes use of it often. But as Dickinson shows, irony may be used to complicate the speaker's feelings without calling their intensity into question.

The most obvious and effective way to use irony in a poem while avoiding a distant tone is to include the speaker as one of the objects of irony. We have already seen an example of this strategy in Dickinson's "I shall know why," in which the speaker turns her mockery outward and inward at the same time:

I shall know why—when Time is over—
And I have ceased to wonder why—
Christ will explain each separate anguish
In the fair schoolroom of the sky—

He will tell me what "Peter" promised—
And I—for wonder at his woe—
I shall forget the drop of Anguish
That scalds me now—that scalds me now!

Overtly the poem declares the speaker's faith in a heavenly consolation for human suffering; covertly it rejects such faith as irrelevant to
present need. The speaker's means of suggesting the covert meaning
are not subtle. She begins, after the first half-line of assertion, by exposing the uselessness of the orthodox Christian promise. Its answers
will come only when she will no longer need them, because she either
no longer exists or no longer suffers as mortals do. And the comic
reduction that the phrase "fair schoolroom" gives to the doctrine of
final illumination suggests that in order to believe in the heaven beyond time one must sacrifice adult reason, become a child in a nega-
tive, secular sense, not a religious one. For the adult, the promises of
the Biblical narrative are fiction, and the Biblical characters, as the
quotation marks around "Peter" suggest, are figures from a children's
pageant. And the final consolation offered takes the form not of an
explanation but a distraction, the forgetting of pain in the presence of
the greater pain of Jesus. But that distraction, the concluding repetition asserts, can do nothing to keep the speaker from feeling abandoned. Her pain is unmitigated in the realm that matters most for
her, the present.

Here we have an ironic voice, but the voice is not that of a cool
skeptic. Faith is being questioned by someone in anguish who feels
cruelly disappointed by what faith can offer. To the extent that we feel

the speaker is speaking as a would-be believer, not as an outsider, the speaker not only throws into doubt the promises of orthodoxy but also exposes her own wish to find traditional promises true. The poem may be read, in other words, as the speaker's failed attempt to console herself with official consolations that she knows are inadequate but is not yet willing to set aside. Though in the first stanza she may see Christ as a schoolteacher whose lessons only a child can believe in, she does seem to regard Christ in the second as having the necessary experience to teach from example. But the authority of Christ's suffering does not prove helpful in relieving her own suffering. Theoretically Christ may be the speaker's redeemer, but experientially he fails. In making the voice of experience the voice of truth, the poem presents the speaker as ruefully admitting her own need for the Christian machinery. She is a would-be self-deceiver mocking her wish to be deceived.

The exposure of self-deception in evidence here is not peculiar to Dickinson's use of irony. It is one of irony's most important functions, and has proven particularly popular with contemporary poets, who tend to shy away from presenting themselves as unimpeachable moral authorities. The perspective may not always be as personal as Dickinson's; the "I" may be a general "we." But the poem is usually directed not at some particular class of the self-deceived but at human nature in general. Here, for example, is Jack Gilbert's dark little poem "Games":

> Imagine if suffering were real.
> Imagine if those old people were afraid of death.
> What if the midget or the girl with one arm
> really felt pain? Imagine how impossible it would be
> to live if some people were
> alone and afraid all their lives.[1]

Overtly the speaker presents the reality of suffering as a fictive hypothesis that if true would make life impossible. Covertly it says painful suffering is all around us. We know that the overt statement is meant ironically not because of any bitter asides, as in Dickinson's poem, but because on its very face the statement that suffering is a fiction is absurd, an absurdity emphasized by the examples offered of people whose suffering is only apparent, not real. However weak our imaginations may be, they allow us to understand that the pain felt by the midget, the girl with one arm, and the lonely and frightened is not make-believe. What is gained by affirming the reality of suffering through an ironic assertion of its opposite is evident if we consider what would be lost in recasting the poem in non-ironic terms. A poem beginning with the lines "Suffering is real; / Old people are afraid of death," would not merely seem naive and self-important in its emphatic declaration of the obvious. It would also miss the central focus of the ironic version, the wish to deny the suffering we see around us, to make believe that it really isn't there. The game that the speaker invites the reader to join, pretending that suffering is real, exposes the game we play in convincing ourselves that people with painful lives do not really feel what we would feel in similar situations. If we didn't play this game of denial, we would be forced to live with the crushing burden of empathy and the painful knowledge that the empathy could never make life fair.

Gilbert's poem offers itself as a script that the speaker invites the reader to share, but it does so without actually particularizing either speaker or reader, so the drama between them has to be inferred. In contemporary poems closer to traditional satire the speaker is placed in a particular dramatic situation that the reader is presumed to recognize as familiar. Sometimes the reader may be addressed as directly as Prufrock does when he invites a "you" to join him on his walk through the city. In other poems the "you" may be addressed indirectly. The irony implies an intimacy with an audience able to catch the covert meaning and accept being implicated in the speaker's evasions. Here is "Fun at Crystal Lake" by Michael Van Walleghen:

After a day of whitecaps
and the threat of tornadoes
the lake turns calm again
a few mayflies begin to hatch
and by late afternoon even
the moon is visible.
      Perhaps
things will work out after all.
Perhaps there will be fireworks
later on, or maybe a barbecue,
and if everyone behaves, maybe
a quick ride just before dark
in the speedboat!
      I hope so.
I like happy endings sometimes
don't you? Take the kid
I caught just yesterday,
for instance, at the beach
across the lake, stalking
a chipmunk with a brick.
       He was
"just having fun" he said
and that was that. No doubt
the people at the fancy lodge
are likewise having fun, especially
the man with the fireworks,
the motorcycle kids,
        and whoever it is
who laughs so hysterically
after each explosion. In any case
what good does it do to worry?
What good did it ever do? Take

this dragonfly for instance
eating a bee
      on a red washcloth
or the man with the speedboat
yelling at his brainless son
again, for walking pigeon-toed
for having a sad face
an ugly lip, a forehead
like his mother's.[2]

Overtly the speaker tells us that the day may turn out well if he doesn't brood about unpleasant details. Covertly he tells us that he has many good reasons to worry. The satire falls in part on those who are "having fun" at the picnic grounds in troubling ways, ways that suggest human brutality: the boy trying to kill a chipmunk with a brick, the violence latent at the "fancy lodge," and the father cursing his son for no good reason. But it also is directed by the speaker at his own attempts to persuade himself that to worry about these episodes is foolish. Whatever their gloomy implications about human nature, there's nothing, he's too quick to announce, that he can do about it. One might as well worry about a dragonfly "eating a bee / on a red washcloth." This concluding bit of fatalism is especially telling, since the effort to argue that the father's yelling at his son is as natural and inevitable as killing among insects is patently unconvincing. Animal parents may chastise their children's behavior, but they don't blame them for looking like their mothers. Only human parents do that, when they are unwilling to face their real problems.

As the speaker exposes his own attempts to avoid the harsh truth, the reader is invited to identify with his self-deception. The opening two stanzas draw us in because we think the speaker is simply disposed to look on the bright side. He hopes for a good end to a holiday that has so far been a disappointment, and we have no reason not to agree with his aside to us that begins the third stanza: "I like happy endings sometimes / don't you?" And because he intervenes to save the chipmunk from the boy with the brick, we are willing to regard him as an agent in "happy endings," not merely a hopeful witness. It's only then that we learn what troubling forms of "having fun" have been chosen by the adults of this little society, what else besides the weather the speaker has witnessed and set aside. Having been led to identify with him, we find it hard not to feel that his ironies are mocking our own excuses as well as his. The poem does not invite us to construct alternatives to going along. Like the poet, we are not going to interfere with the crowd or with the man in the speedboat. We are merely going to try to salvage the day as best we can. And in that attempt we are implicated with the poet in evasion.

Can one write an ironic poem about self-delusion in which the speaker and reader are not themselves implicated? The danger in this mode is sounding morally smug, a particular problem today when one can no longer presume any tradition that allows the poet special claims to insight and virtue. If the object of the irony is mankind in general, then the poet risks sounding self-deluding in holding himself superior to his species. If the object is limited to a particular group or individual, the irony may sound biased or one-sided, the sign of a failure of empathy rather than a sharpness of insight. The second problem is easier to handle, though by no means easy to bring off. Consider the rhetorical problems faced by Tess Gallagher in the following poem, in which a specifically focused irony does not include the poet or reader:

Start Again Somewhere

Don't let her stop you this time, Miguel,
though this isn't your name

and you won't look back
if she calls to you.
For today you are Miguel Ricardo
of the daggers and stallions. Already
you are galloping away
on the great sexual beast
of your refusals.

No, Miguel, it isn't right.
No man who loves truly
should stand for it. And anyway, she
couldn't have cared much, the way she got
prettier and prettier for her own sweet
sake, tossing her hair
from the high arched brows,
looking away.

We've seen her type—the soft mouth
and the set of the head like a dare.
Who could resist?
You only did well to catch yourself
in time. Before your heart
made a mess of it. Before
you did something you could live
to regret.

But we were watching you,
those of us who know better
than to take such chances.
You didn't go too far
and now you've set yourself straight.
And you did it just right, Miguel, taking all
the blame like that so she couldn't

hate you, so she'd have to
think of you the rest of her life
as someone she should have loved better.

You're not young, Miguel, but there's time,
time to find that woman
you adored in your youth, the one
who married the butcher and stayed
in the same town raising his sons, scraping
the maps of blood from his aprons.

All in all we're proud of you.
We see you're no fool.
You wouldn't give something for
nothing. To be a fool
takes devotion of the most pigheaded sort.
You have to want one thing in the wrong place
so badly you make it a way of life.
You forget what it costs.
You forget that others see what it
costs you. And at night

when the butcher's wife
takes her red hands from the water
you are there to kiss them, though you close
your eyes, though secretly
you have galloped away
like the fool you are, but a fool
of your own choosing, wasting
the soft lips of her over
and over in the starved corners.[3]

Overtly the speaker praises the "you" she names "Miguel" for his
shrewdness in leaving the woman who has been vexing him before

she causes him too much trouble, and advises him to seek out the woman more suited to him, the lost love of his youth. Covertly the speaker suggests he has been foolish to reject an actual woman who is worth pursuing for a woman of fantasy. What the real woman has done to offend Miguel is not spelled out, though it's suggested that she has not been as forthcoming in her feelings as he has been, that he has had to court her without clear signs of reciprocity. But the offense that might have roused a more ardent lover to more strenuous courting seems to have both offended his pride and deflated his courage. Instead of finding her archness a challenge, as we might expect of a "Miguel Ricardo" of romantic legend, he stages a proud retreat "on the great sexual beast" of his refusals, and does it in a way that he hopes will make her blame herself for not rising to the occasion. In the last three stanzas, in which the speaker ironically encourages Miguel to dream of rescuing his lost love, it becomes evident that even in his fantasies Miguel can't quite manage to take the action required. Though he can imagine her as the wife of a butcher, who would presumably be grateful for his active intervention, he would rather close his eyes as he kisses her hands, rather imagine kissing her lips in the "starved corners" of some still deeper fantasy of withdrawal from life. Unable to be the holy fool who, in defiance of prudence, makes love a way of life, he is the unholy fool who prefers dreaming to living.

Ironic praise would seem to be just the right technique to mock a fool who thinks he is shrewd, and the poem is very skillful in the way it exposes "Miguel" without ever offering any direct censure. But the poem does encounter an aesthetic problem because of its restricted focus on a single target. The other examples of irony we've examined are more resonant because they deal with a delusion that feels more universal, in good part because the speaker and the reader themselves participate in it. It's true that the direct address to "Miguel" implies familiarity of the poet with her subject, and now and then the poet does seem to suggest she shares Miguel's cautious values, referring to herself as one of "those . . . who know better / than to take . . . chances," but this group is never more than a rhetorical gesture. The speaker does not present herself as sharing in "Miguel's" blindness. Her mockery is focused on him exclusively, as it would not be in a poem in which the speaker felt partly responsible for the delusion that she is mocking. And we might also expect someone remorseful to drop the ironic stance long enough to tell the deluded man directly not to follow the lead of those like her who have claimed to "know better." At the very least the reader would have to be assured that "Miguel" understood the reasons for the attack that was being leveled at him. But here we have no such assurance. For all we know he understands only the overt statement, not the covert critique the poet shares with the reader.

The problem of the speaker's distance in a poem like this is well stated by Kierkegaard in his book on irony, in which he distinguishes between irony and more direct methods of mockery. Both include, he remarks, "an unerring eye for what is crooked, wrong, and vain in existence." But though "irony sees the vanity," he continues, "it diverges in making its observation, because it does not destroy the vanity; it is not what punitive justice is in relation to vice, does not have the redeeming feature of the comic but instead reinforces vanity in its vanity and makes what is lunatic even more lunatic. This is what could be called irony's attempt to mediate the discrete elements—not into a higher unity but into a higher lunacy."[4] Kierkegaard's notion of irony as reinforcement does not seem to apply to the kind of poem in which the speaker includes himself and the reader as part of the satire. But it does seem relevant to a poem like Gallagher's. In encouraging someone she does not mean to enlighten to persist in his error, the speaker risks sounding unfeeling. On the other hand, given the vividness of the speaker's voice, it may be argued that this risk is worth running. However indirect the speaker may be with regard to

Miguel, the reader is likely to be led by the intense focus of the poem to decide that the indirection is the result not of cool detachment but of an effort to control the speaker's anger at Miguel's unshakable self-deceptions. While Miguel is not within the reach of this pointed irony, we readers are, and, by extension, so is the Miguel within us. This defense is forceful to the extent that the reader is persuaded that the speaker's frustrations at Miguel's obtuseness are justified, a conclusion we would be more likely to make if we had a clear indication that the speaker has tried and failed to penetrate Miguel's defenses. Still it's hard to deny the power of the poem. The important task here is not so much to determine the exact degree of its success but to recognize that its success is dependent on its overcoming a significant rhetorical problem.

Most traditional satire that uses irony manages to avoid some of the problems that Gallagher's poem encounters by avoiding the suggestion of any personal connection between the poet and the people ridiculed. At times the poet may presume that the poem will serve an immediate social benefit by chastening fools and knaves, and Pope in the second "Epilogue to the Satires" calls satire a "sacred weapon left for truth's defense, / Sole dread of folly, vice, and insolence" (lines 212–13). But just as often the poet presumes that the world will always contain its share of those who are scorn-proof. Then the business of the poet is to point out foibles or vices in a way that affirms with his audience a shared notion of the difference between good and bad behavior. In one of the great moments of satire in English poetry, the first half of the eighteenth century, that shared ideal was still influenced by notions of self-discipline and civic commitment that derived from Renaissance humanism. The use of irony to promote that ideal presupposed a community of readers who did not require the overt statement of those standards to understand their application. So any literate reader could catch the point of Swift's comparison, in his "De-

scription of a City Shower," between the "beau" in his sedan chair
and the Greeks in the Trojan horse:

> Boxed in a chair the beau impatient sits,
> While spouts run clattering o'er the roof by fits,
> And ever and anon with frightful din
> The leather sounds; he trembles from within.
> So when Troy chairmen bore the wooden steed,
> Pregnant with Greeks impatient to be freed
> (Those bully Greeks, who, as the moderns do,
> Instead of paying chairmen, run them through),
> Laocoon struck the outside with his spear,
> And each imprisoned hero quaked for fear.[5]

This heroic comparison, which pretends to exalt its subject, works, of
course, on our sense of the discrepancy between the unheroic beau
and the Greek warriors, between the dandy afraid that his clothes
will be ruined by the rain, and so make him unfit for his vocation of
charmer and seducer, and the Greek heroes risking their lives to take
Troy and bring home the abducted wife of Menelaus. The only men
who need fear the beau are his tradesmen, whom he destroys by not
paying what he owes them, and so shows himself not merely trivial
but parasitic, though Swift's wit keeps the mockery from sounding
moralistic.

The problem with this kind of irony for modern readers is not that
it is cold but that it seems too easily confined to a definite social type,
to a figure and not a person, and hence does not directly engage the
feelings of the poet and reader. The mock heroic comparison implies
that the subject is ultimately small, a smallness that is underscored
by pretending that it is significant, while we tend to be more at home
today with irony that implies the reverse, that suggests something
significant has been treated as something small, that a difficult truth

has been evaded. So in Dickinson's poem the poet's need for solace is treated as a need for schoolroom instruction; in Gilbert's poem the possibility of human suffering is regarded as a game; in Van Walleghen's poem human cruelty is reduced to "just having fun"; and in Gallagher's poem an evasion of love is presented as shrewdness. I don't want to suggest that mock heroic techniques are no longer available to us, only that they are not likely to be the central device of a poem because they keep the poet too far from the material. They are more likely to exist side by side with other elements that suggest engagement, as part of a dialectic between criticism and affirmation.

This kind of dialectic has always been one of the basic strategies of poetry in the West, so it seems proper to use an example from ancient Rome, Catullus's ironic poem on the death of Lesbia's sparrow:

> Mourn, O Venuses and Cupids,
> And all men of tender feelings.
> My girl's sparrow has died,
> A sparrow, my girl's delight,
> Which she loved more than her own eyes.
> For he was as sweet as honey and knew her
> As well as my girl knew her own mother.
> It did not move from her bosom
> But hopping here and there
> Chirped to its mistress alone.
> But now it travels the way of shadows
> From which, it is said, no one returns.
> Curses on you, you evil shadows of Hell,
> Who devour everything beautiful.
> You have stolen away from me a beautiful sparrow.
> O evil deed! O poor little sparrow!
> For you the eyes of my girl
> Are swollen and red as she cries.[6]

In applying the gestures of the high style, which might be appropriate for the loss of great friend, to the death of the sparrow, the speaker seems to be mocking his sweetheart's sense of proportion. She is taking something small as something grand. But the speaker is also willing to acknowledge a particular closeness between the girl and the sparrow—her familial love for the bird and the sparrow's apparent bonding to the girl—so that while mocking her excessive grief he is also showing a capacity to sympathize. If he does not share his sweetheart's pain, he's sorry for the real pain she is feeling. And the poem ends not with ironic gestures but with a lover's observation that his sweetheart's eyes are red and swollen, with a sad fact that can't be laughed away.

In a poem both mocking and tender at once, critical and yet affirming, Catullus is using irony to define one voice in a dialectic that expands the genre of the love poem. In modern versions of this technique, in which opposed tonalities are juxtaposed in more radical ways, the notion of genre itself may be open to question. When irony occurs in such a poem, it is "unstable," to borrow Wayne Booth's term, in that meaning cannot be determined by simple reversal of the overt statement.[7] The overt meaning is clearly meant to be rejected, but the covert meaning does not immediately reveal itself. It has to be pieced together by a reader open to the tensions between discrete perspectives. I think we can recognize this kind of irony immediately in a poem like Allen Ginsberg's well-known "America." The opening lines make clear its methods:

> America I've given you all and now I'm nothing.
> America two dollars and twentyseven cents January 17, 1956.
> I can't stand my own mind.
> America when will we end the human war?
> Go fuck yourself with your atom bomb.
> I don't feel good don't bother me.

I won't write my poem till I'm in my right mind.

America when will you be angelic?

When will you take off your clothes?

When will you look at yourself through the grave?

When will you be worthy of your million Trotskyites?

America why are your libraries full of tears?

America when will you send your eggs to India?

I'm sick of your insane demands.

When can I go into the supermarket and buy what I need with
my good looks?

America after all it is you and I who are perfect not the next
world.

Your machinery is too much for me.

You made me want to be a saint.

There must be some other way to settle this argument.

Burroughs is in Tangiers I don't think he'll come back it's
sinister.

Are you being sinister or is this some form of practical joke?

I'm trying to come to the point.

I refuse to give up my obsession.

America stop pushing I know what I'm doing.

America the plum blossoms are falling.[8]

As we read these lines we are forced to keep readjusting our notion
of the poet's intentions. The first five lines seem to establish a tone of
angry protest against an America that has reduced the poet to penury
and, as line 3 suggests, to self-contempt. The rulers of America, while
obsessed with fictitious external threats, have in fact engaged in a war
against their own people. But the sixth line gives us pause because it
suggests that the poet's problems may be more personal than political
("I don't feel good") and that he is not so much outraged by America as merely "bothered" by it, and wants simply to be left alone.

Apparently he does not want to write an attack on America at all or rather, the next line tells us, wants to wait till he is in his "right mind," though this decision does not keep him from continuing. We seem to have a poem with two distinct voices, one outraged, one merely disgruntled, one out to attack political failure, one whose purposes are more difficult to define. And the next six lines, each of which asks a question, sharpens this duality. The last four questions seem to involve a return to the initial voice of political accusation, attacking America for serving death, for being unworthy of its idealists and indifferent to the suffering in other countries. But the first two—

> America when will you be angelic?
> When will you take off your clothes?

—present a speaker who makes political demands that are comically inappropriate. Even an ardent idealist would not be likely to expect a country to be "angelic," and what would it mean for America to go without clothes? The lines call into question the appropriateness of the poem's basic device of addressing a country as a person. Here the poet seems to be mocking himself for his own idealistic excess, an excess that he pointedly returns to after the more serious questions:

> I'm sick of your insane demands.
> When can I go into the supermarket and buy what I need with
>   my good looks?

In these lines, the tone of protest, which in the opening seemed heartfelt, sounds wholly ironic. The poet matches the "insane demands" of America with his own absurdities, enjoying a clownish piece of poetic narcissism. The juxtaposition of solemnity with ironic play makes the reader regard the poem as a kind of stage in which two different poetic intentions—the would-be protest poem and the would-be poem of self-mocking comedy—are allowed to struggle for center stage. In the concluding lines of the passage I've quoted, the poet does seem to settle for a kind of synthesis, presenting himself as someone aware of his own obsessions who is trying to talk a somewhat distant acquaintance, who is not aware of his own deeper irrationalities, into a peaceable enjoyment of life. If "America" can give up postponing its joys for some future life—"America after all it is you and I who are perfect not the next world"—step away from its fears, and "stop pushing" in its rush to the future, then it may notice the simple beauties passing away before its eyes: "America the plum blossoms are falling." But while the poet struggles to be sweetly reasonable he is also being absurd. How is modern America going to be transformed into a gentleman of old Japan ready to meditate with the poet among the plum blossoms?

The contradictory genres that "America" seems to be written in can be traced back to the poet's making contradictory claims. Its irony exists, as it does in all the poems we have looked at so far, in the tonal complexities of a single voice. An alternative form of irony, most common in drama and dramatic monologue, is produced by the difference between the speaker's attitude and the poet's, between, say, the way Browning's Duke of Ferrara sees himself and the way the poet sees him. Because I am interested in this book in rhetorical strategies with which poets can fashion their own voices, I have focused here on tonal irony, not dramatic. But it might be useful to look at one special case of dramatic irony that raises the question of genre. At the center of this kind of irony is a catalog, without commentary, of various examples of debased speech. Drama here is generated by the conflict between the kind of language we expect to find in the poem, a personal language purified of the clichés of the tribe, and the undigested boluses of media-speak that suggest that the traditional poem may no longer be possible. Charles Bernstein is one of the best practitioners of this genre. Here is part of a single section from his long poem "Emotions of Normal People":

I'd like you to meet Jane Franham.
Jane was my mother-in-law until I married
Jim. While I was sure of Joan's
love, I still
worried that she might be tempted
by other men. Now both hands
are able to work, since the magnifier
is suspended around
the neck on an adjustable length of
cord. We had argued about his
job before, about how wrong it was for a man with three kids
to spend so few days a year
at home, with
no end in sight. I
suspect your father had an adrenal
gland tumor that was
driving his blood pressure
up. Lillie was very emphatic that she
wanted to be a ballet dancer; the nun thing
was just a passing
phase that lots of girls
go through. Lipstick
is meant to be the perfect
finishing touch—one that doesn't
compete with
your eyeshadow or clash
with your blushes.
Only
when the soup course
is finished is
the service plate
taken out.— *Who's the woman* YOU
most admire? Is it

Shirley Temple Black, Raisa Gorbachev, Phyllis
Schlafly, Winnie Mandela, Mother Teresa of
Calcutta, or Ella Fitzgerald?
After my neck surgery, Marge asked me
if I would be
investing in a lot of scarves.
The Cowley's
one exceptional
expenditure is the $583 they give every month
to their church.
. . . .
However you come to terms
with your feelings about your husband, you must
face the fact that your son is totally
innocent of any
responsibility. No matter how much bitterness
his father deserves, you must not transfer it
to the boy. Define
brows with
brown eye-shadow
pencil; blend with
stiff brow brush
for natural
effect.[9]

We have here a splicing together of various kinds of formulaic discourse. "Discourse" seems a more precise word than "speeches" because we can't feel any actual person standing behind the lines. Some
of the sentences do seem to be bits of actual conversation, but these
bits are interwoven with clippings from user manuals, etiquette books,
teenage magazines, local church newspapers, and self-help guides to
everyday psychology, suggesting that the conversation is cut from
the same impersonal cloth. The jumbling together of these fragments

suggests the welter of pseudo communication that one is likely to be pelted with during a day. What is most evident about this kind of irony, when approached from the poems we've looked at here, is that it is not contained in the poet's own voice. The poet has chosen rather to absent himself from the poem, or to be indirectly present only as the compiler of an exhibit that explains his absence. With the language so contaminated and corrupted, the poem suggests, the safest kind of poem to write is a catalog of misuse that makes clear the difficulties that any genuine attempt at communication is up against. The contrast with Ginsberg's "America" is instructive. The speaker in that poem believes he can actually talk things through with "America" and jolly it out of its craziness, though he laughs at himself for his own presumptions. But in Bernstein's poem the problem has moved from stubborn mindsets to the medium itself, which can't be used without cheapening any subject it touches. Some glimmer of hope may be provided by the epigraph from Adorno that heads the poem: "Truth is the antithesis of existing society"; but that antithesis might itself be in danger if it lapses further into language. The only truth available seems to be mockery, though that weapon can do little to check the tide of bad language that engulfs us. It certainly offers no protection against the kind of smug dismissal expressed in the lines of pseudo psychology that end the poem:

> In any case, sarcasm
> is evidence of a sadistic trend in one's
> personality.

Many contemporary poets would probably agree with Bernstein about the danger that debased speech presents to genuine communication, but most are not as radically gloomy about the power of the poet to resist it. They would argue that the danger only makes it more important for poets to try to keep their own language free of cant as they go about making contemporary formulations of the truths they consider significant. When they use irony in their poems, they use it often against themselves, working to provide a countervoice to their own traditional wish to make affirmations. The irony does not finally cancel the affirmation; it only suggests that the poet realizes that the will to affirm is based more on stubborn hope than on an empirical study of human history. For my example of this dialectic, I choose a poem by Czeslaw Milosz, which, like the poem by Adam Zagajewski that closed the first chapter, suggests an awareness of the limits of poetry that does not lose faith in what poetry can do. Here is Robert Pinsky's translation of Milosz's "Incantation":

Human reason is beautiful and invincible.
No bars, no barbed wire, no pulping of books,
No sentence of banishment can prevail against it.
It establishes the universal ideas in language,
And guides our hand so we write Truth and Justice
With capital letters, lie and oppression with small.
It puts what should be above things as they are,
Is an enemy of despair and a friend of hope.
It does not know Jew from Greek or slave from master,
Giving us the estate of the world to manage.
It saves austere and transparent phrases
From the filthy discord of tortured words.
It says that everything is new under the sun,
Opens the congealed fist of the past.
Beautiful and very young are Philo-Sophia
And poetry, her ally in the service of the good.
As late as yesterday Nature celebrated their birth,
The news was brought to the mountains by a unicorn and an echo.
Their friendship will be glorious, their time has no limit.
Their enemies have delivered themselves to destruction.[10]

The poem seems ironical because the overt assertions about reason are too good to be true, too visionary to be presented in the declarative, unqualified manner that the speaker assumes. By overstating his case the poet would seem to be ridiculing all those who would believe, in defiance of history, that there exists such a thing as human reason that we can all agree about, that it points us to ideals everyone shares, that it discriminates between a true and corrupt formulation of these ideals, and that when aided by poetry its power is irresistible. The covert mockery becomes overt near the end, in which reason's love of the truth and poetry's serving of that love are presented as "news . . . brought to the mountains by a unicorn and an echo." Only in myth will these two figures be triumphant. But if the assertions of the poem are all ironic, the meaning of the poem does not lie in their negation, in an assertion that human reason is partial, confused, time-serving, and powerless. Myth may not be validated by history, but it does validate the persistence of human wishes. This poet, like all poets, believes that history should not be given the last word, that truth is a goddess worshipped by everyone of good will, that poetry is meant to serve her by praising what might be rather than what is, that at its most inspired it reaches across the divisions of class and place and time to express insights that are universally valid and vital. If the speaker laughs at such absurd belief, he laughs at himself, for the poem he has written, despite its qualifications, is still one more example of that belief in action, an "incantation" meant to make the hoped-for ideal a reality. Irony here, rather than undermining his assertions, works to make them possible. Reason with a small "r" laughs at reason with a capital "r" but does not offer itself as a substitution, only as a recognition that its greater brother dwells in possibility rather than in fact, possibility that, as Dickinson tells us, is a "fairer house than prose."

CHAPTER FOUR

Political Poetry

THE ASSOCIATION in the previous chapter of irony with satire led us to examine a few poems that take on public concerns. Irony has proven a time-honored technique for dealing with political issues in a way that avoids easy pieties and solemnities. But even with this tradition available, particular difficulties with the genre have led to a dearth of successful political poetry in America today. Part of the problem may stem from the belief that public issues are inherently unpoetical, a notion that has its classic American formulation in the aestheticism of Poe that pits truth against beauty and defines beauty as "the sole province of the poem." The cure for this narrowing of topic may lie simply in turning to a more enlightened poetics, to the injunctions, say, of Emerson and Whitman that encourage poets to enlarge their interests as much as possible. But certain rhetorical problems peculiar to the genre are also responsible for making it hard going. What I want to do here is discuss some of these problems in a way that suggests how successful poems overcome them.

The most common kind of failure in political poetry involves party thinking. Public issues invite combative orthodoxies, with approved arguments and opinions. And poets who are not careful can easily be tempted to become advocates for a group rather than for themselves alone. The result is writing that sounds too much like propaganda—

strident and preachy in tone, derivative in language, and predictable in outlook. Such a poem can't persuade because it seems to have no one in particular standing behind it, no one willing to reject ready-made ideas and discover on his own what he actually believes. The temptations to party thinking are especially strong in the kind of political poem most likely to have been written in America for the last forty years, an expression of disaffection with the politics of our political leaders and the values of the people who've elected them. Though one might assume that dissent would be less monolithic than orthodoxy, in practice poets who see themselves as members of a beleaguered minority tend to band together for safety and support. And even those outside a formal group may feel reluctant to use language that the group might find unfamiliar or offensive.

Every good writer has his own way of making public subjects his own, but the one strategy good writers share is to present speakers who try to be honest about the limits of their positions, who recognize that the best political choices are not ideal, that they are reached by compromising with intractable facts, that the good they bring is often accompanied by some harm. Such concessions are hard to make when the writer feels outraged by some particularly offensive public wrong, but being hard-won they are all the more powerful, and help to make a poem's assertions particularly convincing. Consider the way the speaker in Philip Lopate's poem "Allende" manages to express his indignation at the overthrow of the Allende regime in Chile without lapsing into political rhetoric:

In 200 years they won't remember me, Salvador
And they won't remember you, so let's skip the part about
He will live with us forever.
You may get a footnote for being the only Marxist
To gain power in Latin America via parliamentary means;
And the only sucker not to throw his enemies in jail.

You knew the power of the large land-owners, ITT,
The Army, U.S. Anaconda, the small frightened businessmen
Easily manipulated, the shop-owners who could go either way
And yet you didn't lift a finger to silence them.
You continued to defend the bicameral system of government
Until they bombed your palace and you shot yourself in the mouth.
Answer me this,
Now that you are a bunch of hairs on a blood-stained sofa:
I want to know why you killed yourself.
Because this was a very un-Marxist thing to do.
Because neither was this the way of a gradualist
With short graying hair and glasses, and a face like a prominent
    surgeon's,
Who, knowing this would happen, could have easily arranged for
The secret tunnel, the private plane, the unmarked car
In which you, huddled in grandmotherly wig, might begin
To write your memoirs. Was it too horrible to think of
Speaking at New York rallies to pockets of émigrés,
Forming shadow cabinets, and lunching with Juan Bosch
Or Andreas Papandreou, swapping stories over wine about
Where you were when the shit hit the fan?
I'm being vulgar, forgive me.
I would rather believe in your doggish retreat
Than the flamboyance of today's headlines which gloat:
MARXIST REPORTED TO TAKE HIS LIFE.
Even they are a little unsure. They leave room for the graduate students
Of the left, working in the carrels of libraries
For 100 years to discover the link,
The way it all fits together: Lumumba, King, Kennedy, Allende, CIA.

And it may turn out that my government actually murdered you
But what's the good of knowing that?

We know too many connections already, and they only satisfy
The pedantic urge that makes the world a crossword puzzle.
Salvador, I'm sorry, I don't know what to say any more.
Take back the bullet, it was a mistake, it redeems nothing.

Today I look at the faces of passers-by and I think:
It figures. The banks have the money to buy counterrevolution,
This wino has no money. He's nice enough, so is
That girl in the flamingo summer dress on wobbly heels.
It's September 12, possibly the prettiest day of the year.
The blue has never been so pure around the chimneys—
"Almost like—a cartoon!" says the dental hygienist,
Grasping for a metaphor. I never said it even to myself,
Before today, but just between you and me,
And I don't want anyone else to hear:
                                    Señor,
It looks as if they have got us by the balls.
These faces in the street, how can they take power?
How can they rule? [1]

   The speaker here immediately wins our confidence because his
elegy for Allende begins by dismissing the political pieties that the
genre invites. Though Allende's death stirs him to write, he is distant
enough from his feelings to acknowledge that Allende's rule was too
brief and ineffectual to secure more than a passing mention in the
history books. The tone is irreverent, with elements of admiration,
anger, affection, and confusion mixed together in shifting propor-
tions as the speaker tries to make sense of Allende's death. Allende is
both a man of principle and a "sucker" who tries to defend strict
democracy and a respect for law in impossible circumstances. He is
not a hero whose life inspires followers. He is only an undignified
"bunch of hairs on a blood-stained sofa." Yet he is alive enough to be

mocked, chided, lectured, and pleaded with as the poet questions him about his suicide. The poet can't help satirizing Allende for behavior that repudiates the doctrines of Marxism and gradualism, but the hurt behind the mockery is clear as he turns even more scorn on the life that would have awaited Allende as an expatriate, and then on the false neutrality of the *Times* headline. This mixture of feelings, which provides much of the dramatic interest of the poem, is never resolved. Allende's commitment to democratic ideals is both commendable and impractical. His suicide, whether prompted by despair or a proud contempt for the indignities of exile, "redeems nothing," and the poet, instead of voicing hope in the possibilities of political renewal, merely wishes that the act could be undone.

Besides resisting the official rhetoric of praise, the poem also manages not to demonize Allende's enemies. Though the speaker's disgust with them is obvious, their guilt becomes the given of the poem rather than its central focus. The poet has moved from what may be called the first-order question of who is guilty to the second-order question of what sense can be made of Allende's failure. He is too involved with Allende to concoct a grand theory of conspiracy:

> And it may turn out that my government actually murdered you
> But what's the good of knowing that?
> We know too many connections already, and they only satisfy
> The pedantic urge that makes the world a crossword puzzle.

By keeping the focus on Allende, rather than on his enemies, the speaker manages to work through enough of his frustration so that by the end of the poem he can see Allende, with all his contradictions, as an alter ego, a brotherly confidant with whom he shares a similar political plight. For the poet also lives in a country where ordinary people have little power and where a revolution in the name of democracy has ultimately failed. And the cause is not a coup sponsored by the army, or landowners, or foreign investors, that would justify the Manichaean rhetoric of the victim, but a more basic failure in the ideal of democracy itself, a misplaced faith in the ability of people to govern themselves. "We the people" turn out, in the powerful and witty closing lines, to be "nice enough" but not the kind of citizens that are required to keep a country free. They lack the required understanding and commitment. The tone is not scornful here, more comically rueful and tender, but the implications of the final question—"How can they rule?"—are devastating.

"Allende" exemplifies one way of writing a moving political poem free of the conventional language of praise and blame. But its irreverent and bitter tone raises another question about contemporary political poetry that is harder to deal with than the problem of party language, the presumption of the powerlessness of the individual. Lopate's speaker can move closer in sympathy to Allende as he wrestles with the implications of Allende's fate, but the understanding brings no transforming power. Allende's death does not shake the speaker out of his ironies. It "redeems nothing," unlike the death, say, of the rebels in Yeats's "Easter, 1916," which allows its speaker to move from the cynicism of the "casual comedy" of typical Irish politics to the celebration of heroic achievement. Allende's death only confirms the conviction of Lopate's speaker that nothing can change. And his final lesson for Allende is that neither of them can do anything against the greed of the strong and the indifference of the weak. This sense of the incapacity of the individual to make a significant difference in public life helps explain why even poets who have little difficulty in avoiding public rhetoric are often reluctant to deal with political issues in their work. Poetry has traditionally been founded on the faith that the poem can clarify life in ways that make both writer and reader more free, that it can uphold beleaguered ideals and suggest how they might be embodied in the world. But if the poet no longer believes that justice can be embodied in a political order and still wants to be true to the traditional functions of poetry, he may feel impelled to turn to the private realm where the individual still does have power. The alternative would seem to be poetry of passive shrugs and crippling ironies.

Does "Allende" make us feel in fact like powerless participants in the casual comedy of American politics? I think that for at least some readers its overt theme of powerlessness is countered to some extent by the strongly defined speaker, whose anger, hurt, and confusion enact a ritual of concern that ultimately serves as a model for lonely commitment. The speaker knows that his emotional investments are doomed to be frustrated, but he does not present himself finally as a mocker of ideals. And if the poet closes with an expression of hopelessness about the possibility of real democracy, the speaker's disappointment makes clear that he and Allende form a beleaguered community of two, the last two noble fools who care about a liberty that seems destined never to be embodied. In speaking as a moral man in an immoral world, Lopate's speaker can in fact be placed in the tradition of political satire that begins with Juvenal's lonely invective at the corruption of imperial Rome, though Lopate denies himself Juvenal's nostalgia for the manly virtues of the old Republic. The speaker in "Allende" does not look back to a better past to expose the present. He seems to read Allende's failure simply as another example of the continual failure of democratic hopes. But the attack on America as a colonial power inevitably reminds us how far we've come from the colony we once were, how we are now inflicting on others the kind of injuries we once considered intolerable. Allende's quixotic defense of the "bicameral legislature" suggests, in fact, that he has borrowed some of his ideas from the constitution of the country that has worked to ruin him.

Lopate's voice of lonely virtue resists powerlessness by naming the forces against it, but this form of resistance might still seem too restrictive and concessive for writers used to the latitude of the personal lyric, where the poet can be shaken out of old modes of thought and enter into larger dispensations. Lopate's satiric voice, noble in its honesty, can't manage any faith in political transformation. And this sense of diminishment of possibility is especially vivid for Americans because of the expansive, visionary element that is clearly present in the work of Whitman, perhaps our greatest political poet. *Leaves of Grass* offers its readers the possibility of a new social order based not on law but on the sympathy of free individuals who have managed to throw off the rigid hierarchies of Europe for an unconfined openness to experience. Though we can't accept its hopeful vision today without feeling naive about the weight of American history, the language of the *Leaves* is so stirring, the voice so engaging, cunning, and witty, that we can't be sure if we suffer from darker experience or diminished inspiration.

If we want to be honest about our doubts about America but also want to resist satiric ironies for the loftier rhetoric of praise and blame associated with epic or tragedy, we might want to consider the example of Ginsberg's "Howl," which deliberately risks melodrama in order to avoid restricting the poem's scope. Ginsberg's "best minds," crazed drifters with no place in the social order, make unlikely heroes. But his wish to celebrate them seems more important than the wish to chronicle what has been wasted:

> I saw the best minds of my generation destroyed by madness,
>   starving hysterical naked,
> dragging themselves through the negro streets at dawn looking for
>   an angry fix.
> angelheaded hipsters burning for the ancient heavenly connection
>   to the starry dynamo in the machinery of night,
> who poverty and tatters and hollow-eyed and high sat up smoking
>   in the supernatural darkness of cold-water flats floating across
>   the tops of cities contemplating jazz,
> who bared their brains to Heaven under the El and saw

Mohammedan angels staggering on tenement roofs illuminated,
who passed through universities with radiant cool eyes
    hallucinating Arkansas and Blake-light tragedy among the
    scholars of war,
who were expelled from the academies for crazy & publishing
    obscene odes on the windows of the skull,
who cowered in unshaven rooms in underwear, burning their
    money in wastebaskets and listening to the Terror through
    the wall.[2]

The protagonists' fits of mania and despair, their frantic travel, their compulsive drug-taking and sexual promiscuity, are presented less as symptoms of collapse than as part of a noble effort to reach illumination, to take Blake's road of excess to the palace of wisdom. Though the "best minds" ultimately fail to make any sustaining contact with a liberating truth, they exemplify a spirit of the Romantic quester whose nobility makes ordinary life seem by comparison shallow and sterile. The speaker of "Howl," unlike the speaker in Lopate's poem, is not tempted to mock his subjects for their Quixotic hopes, though to the jaundiced eye their projects of spiritual transformation are far more nebulous and illusory than Allende's faith in democratic politics. However fitful their insights, their excesses are still important as testimony to their resistance to the falseness of ordinary life. The poem's refusal to adopt a critical perspective is embodied stylistically in the use of the catalog as its main mode of development. Though at first the starkness of the street images seems to be meant as an ironic contrast to Whitman's desire to praise, the ultimate effect of the discontinuous listing is to suggest a view of the spiritual life as a series of discontinuous moments of insight, moments to which traditional narrative, with its assumptions about causal sequence, cannot do justice.

Is the poem successful in convincing us of the nobility of the "best minds," in making us believe that they are the priests of a visionary order that has struggled and failed to be born? Not completely, it seems to me, even though the imaginative and emotional energy of the poem is impressive: its surprising juxtapositions, its voice of passionate concern grounded in vivid images. The chief problem is that the speaker does not raise any questions about the heroes' failure that would be likely to occur to a detached observer. Why, we may ask, were the "best minds" unable to discover less self-destructive forms of spiritual questing? The poet does appear to deal with this issue in the second section, in his diatribe against Moloch, but he never explains how this modern god of *cupiditas* could have destroyed his heroes if they remained, as we are led to believe they managed to, uncontaminated by its values. The speaker vents his rage against Moloch in abstract terms that do not make the connection clear:

> What sphinx of cement and aluminum bashed open their skulls and
>   ate up their brains and imagination?
> Moloch! Solitude! Filth! Ugliness! Ashcans and unobtainable dollars!
>   Children screaming under the stairways! Boys sobbing in armies!
>   Old men weeping in the parks!
> Moloch! Moloch! Nightmare of Moloch! Moloch the loveless!
>   Mental Moloch! Moloch the heavy judger of men!
> Moloch the incomprehensible prison! Moloch the crossbone
>   soulless jailhouse and Congress of sorrows! Moloch whose
>   buildings are judgment! Moloch the vast stone of war! Moloch
>   the stunned governments!
> Moloch whose mind is pure machinery! Moloch whose blood is
>   running money! Moloch whose fingers are ten armies! Moloch
>   whose breast is a cannibal dynamo! Moloch whose ear is a
>   smoking tomb!

Moloch here is presented as a demonic power, the fit adversary for the hero of epic or romance. But Ginsberg gives us no occasion that pits his dragon against his knights in open combat. We are introduced to the "best minds" when they have already been broken in battles that have presumably taken place offstage. We may be able to pity these losers, but it's hard to identify with them because they are given no real choices. In making his heroes helpless victims, Ginsberg has inadvertently deprived them of their dignity.

As is the case with Lopate's "Allende," what keeps "Howl" from sounding defeatist is the strong voice of the speaker, who has clearly not been crushed by Moloch, who mourns the "best minds" and attacks their enemies with a howl of lament and accusation that is closer in spirit to Jeremiah than to Lamentations. How useful this prophetic model can be for poets writing today is not an easy question to answer. It seems to be a version of that American bardic spirit that animates poets as different as Whitman and Pound, which, when successfully embodied, can produce an exhilaration not possible in less ambitious poems. But even if a speaker in this mode manages to avoid sounding uncritical in his praise and blame, he still may sound morally naive, lacking in self-awareness, because of the tendency of the bard to assume that the enemy is outside himself, not within. So Ginsberg's poet speaks only in one line of his own battling with Moloch, and the battle seems to have been already won:

> Moloch who entered my soul early! Moloch in whom I am a
> consciousness without a body! Moloch who frightened me out of
> my natural ecstasy! Moloch whom I abandon!

The same problem of moral remoteness is evident even in Lopate's "Allende." The speaker's witty self-deprecation keeps him from sounding self-righteous, but his bitter idealism leads him to distance himself from everyone but Allende. The readers of the poem, on the other hand, are likely to find themselves mirrored not only in the right-thinking solitary speaker but also in the innocuous citizens he meets on the street, who abet the wrongdoing of their government by ignorance and indifference. The voice of lonely virtue, in other words, avoids the feeling of shame that is one of the most common conditions of any citizen in a powerful democracy who feels that his country is doing evil in his name. Such shame is the inevitable starting point for much political poetry today. The feeling isn't purely rational, for it seems to blur important distinctions in degrees of complicity. We are not in any logical sense responsible for all the wrongs committed in our name. And shame can have the unhappy result of leading either to a withdrawal from political identifications or to fruitless rituals of self-flagellation. But it does make some sense in terms of what might be called the logic of the will, the will that attempts to assert responsibility for as much as it can, to see the self as an agent rather than as a helpless victim. If we are to write useful political poetry, we have to figure out how to begin with shame and then move beyond confessions of failure, affirming the power to give some shape to our lives.

One way to carry out this project without seeming to claim too much power or authority is to place public issues in private contexts. In a poem with such a strategy, the speaker becomes a fully defined character with his own, nonpolitical problems, which are clarified and enlarged by the incursion of the political material. Though this kind of poem may be more narrow in its focus, it exemplifies the way political issues actually come to us in life, as events from the outside for which we make room in our private worlds, and so enacts certain habits of mind that are of real importance if we are to widen our interests beyond ourselves. And by drawing analogies between political problems that seem too large for individual effort and problems where the individual can be expected to have some control, the poem may suggest new possibilities for action.

For many writers of political poetry today who take this approach, Lowell is one of the important immediate influences. Here is his elegy "For Robert Kennedy 1925–1968," which is remarkable for its blending of personal and public concerns:

Here in my workroom, in its listlessness
of Vacancy, like the old townhouse we shut for summer,
airtight and sheeted from the sun and smog,
far from the hornet yatter of his gang—
is loneliness, a thin smoke thread of vital
air. But what will anyone teach you now?
Doom was woven in your nerves, your shirt,
woven in the great clan; they too were loyal,
and you too were loyal to them, to death.
For them like a prince, you daily left your tower
to walk through dirt in your best cloth. Untouched,
alone in my Plutarchan bubble, I miss
you, you out of Plutarch, made by hand—
forever approaching your maturity.[3]

If we approach this poem after reading Lopate's "Allende," we are struck first by the way the poem seems to subordinate Kennedy to the poet's broodings about the frustrations of his own vocation. This speaker is not gripped by grief and anger at Kennedy's death. He is emotionally insulated, his remoteness objectified literally by the distance of the workroom from the "hornet yatter" of Kennedy's public life. This removal is called into question by Kennedy's death. The poet's life suddenly seems empty and lonely as the speaker contrasts his own reclusion with Kennedy's deliberate choice to leave his "tower" of privilege and take up practical work in the world. The strength of such a personal focus is its making the poet's concern with Kennedy wholly credible in psychological terms. We don't have to presume any special involvement of the speaker in American politics, only his predilection toward self-analysis. The danger is that the contrast he draws between Kennedy and himself might lead him into a self-absorbed recrimination that would further isolate him from public life. But the speaker avoids this temptation by deliberately turning outward to Kennedy.

He justifies his contemplative distance in the only way possible, by using it to help him reach a definition of Kennedy's career that would be difficult for someone immersed in the world. Though the poet mocks himself for being "untouched . . . in [his] Plutarchan bubble," he links himself by these words to a tradition of writers who try seriously to understand the lives of those immersed in history. And the concluding description of Kennedy as a figure "out of Plutarch" suggests that this approach does not violate the subject. The lapidary formulation of the last two lines indicates that the poet has clarified, at least for himself, one of the implications of Kennedy's life, and the inclusion of incompleteness in that formulation suggests the writer's awareness that all such summaries have to be qualified.

For Lowell the use of personal material in a political poem helped overcome a tendency in his work toward dry, cynical detachment. It brought him into a world he might otherwise have been content to anatomize from a distance. The movement is famously enacted in "Skunk Hour," as the cool satirist of the first part of the poem, who leads us leisurely through his emblematic tour of cultural decline, is suddenly replaced by the anguished participant who finds "hell" within himself. We can't say that the detachment is merely a screen for private pain, but the stark juxtaposition does suggest that both are aspects of a kindred moral illness and that the cool tone of the opening is not the best way to confront it. However we interpret the skunks at the end of the poem, they appear as both inward and outward presences, their menace and their promise partly the responsibility of the poet.

A personal focus, then, can save a poem both from grandiloquent claims and from remoteness, but it does run one important risk: being too private a response to a public event. "I miss you," says Lowell's speaker to the dead Robert Kennedy, as if Kennedy were merely a figure from the poet's private life, not a figure of national importance. Lowell is careful to provide a context for this sentiment so that it can be read as part of the speaker's efforts to move out of himself to the larger world, but in poems more emphatically self-involved such a context may be inadequately provided. Political material included to enlarge the private sphere may then be itself diminished to a mere backdrop for the private action. A good example of the problem can be found in Sylvia Plath's much-anthologized "Daddy," in which the speaker tries to enlarge her relation to her father by drawing analogies to the relations between the Jews and the Nazis in World War II. Here is the most troubling passage:

> I never could talk to you.
> The tongue stuck in my jaw.
>
> It stuck in a barb wire snare.
> Ich, ich, ich, ich,
> I could hardly speak.
> I thought every German was you.
> And the language obscene
>
> An engine, an engine
> Chuffing me off like a Jew.
> A Jew to Dachau, Auschwitz, Belsen.
> I began to talk like a Jew.
> I think I may well be a Jew.
>
> The snows of the Tyrol, the clear beer of Vienna
> Are not very pure or true.
> With my gipsy ancestress and my weird luck
> And my Taroc pack and my Taroc pack
> I may be a bit of a Jew.
>
> I have always been scared of *you*,
> With your Luftwaffe, your gobbledygoo.
> And your neat mustache

And your Aryan eye, bright blue.
Panzer-man, panzer-man, O You—

Not God but a swastika
So black no sky could squeak through.
Every woman adores a Fascist,
The boot in the face, the brute
Brute heart of a brute like you.[4]

It's hard to read this passage without feeling that the speaker is trying to inflate the importance of her own suffering by claiming identity
with the far greater suffering of others. The rhetoric is strong enough
to make us feel that the speaker believes what she's saying, that her
hate is genuine. But the claim of equivalence is so hyperbolic that its
effect is to undermine the speaker's credibility as a reliable witness of
her own history. This effect is intensified by the lack of any specifics
about what the father has done to provoke the speaker's anger. Without any facts, we have no way of judging the validity of the speaker's claims to mistreatment. Though we seem to be asked to identify
the speaker with the poet, we are likely to feel that we are reading a
dramatic monologue where the speaker's judgment of herself differs
greatly from our own. This difference is especially pronounced at the
end of the poem when the poet claims to have rid herself of her father's power over her. Her ability to express her anger may be a step
in the right direction, but the metaphor of Jew and Nazi suggests how
mythically potent her father still remains, and the speaker can only
declare her freedom by a final mythologizing of herself as a heroic
killer of vampires. Here is a poem, then, whose speaker seems unable to step back from her life and make crucial discriminations. The
political material that might in theory provide some saving distance
seems in fact to be only another symptom of her self-encapsulation.
As a result, we feel that the story of the speaker's relation to her father

is yet to be told, and that the telling will require someone less eager to see herself as a victim of large historical forces and more willing to raise the issue of why she has allowed her father, dead for twenty years, to continue to govern her psychic life. The issue of her complicity is raised in passing at the end of the quoted passage, but only to be avoided by throwing the blame for her submission onto the backs of women in general: "Every woman adores a Fascist." The bad faith involved in the use of this sexist stereotype is only more evidence of the continuing power of her father and her own reluctance to assume some responsibility for her past. How much harder on herself is Plath's speaker in her truly powerful poems like "Tulips," "Candles," "Nick and the Candlestick," and "Last Words," in which the speaker's wish to see herself as victim is resisted by a desire to control her fate as much as she can.

The problems of "Daddy" should not lead the writer of personal poems to shy away from efforts to enlarge the subject with political material, only to avoid using this material to make exaggerated claims for the sufferings of the speaker. Handled with care, it can give the poem a rich resonance by suggesting that what the individual does in his own world has social implications, that private acts help determine the shape of a *polis*. Consider the effects of a political frame on Tony Hoagland's poem about the betrayal of a friendship, "My Country":

When I think of what I know about America,
I think of kissing my best friend's wife
in the parking lot of the zoo one afternoon,

just over the wall from the lion's cage.
One minute making small talk, the next
my face was moving down to meet her

wet and open, upturned mouth. It was a kind of patriotic act,
pledging our allegiance to the pleasure
and not the consequence, crossing over the border

of what we were supposed to do,
burning our bridges and making our bed
to an orchestra of screaming birds

and the smell of elephant manure. Over her shoulder
I could see the sun, burning palely in the winter sky
and I thought of my friend, who always tries

to see the good in situations—how an innocence
like that shouldn't be betrayed.
Then she took my lower lip between her teeth,

I slipped my hand inside her shirt and felt
my principles blinking out behind me
like streetlights in a town where I had never

lived, to which I never intended to return.
And who was left to speak of what had happened?
And who would ever be brave, or lonely,

or free enough to ask?[5]

    The political frame of this poem turns what might have been a simple confession of personal failure into an analogue for the failure of American society as a whole. The speaker isn't trying to excuse his weakness by suggesting its pervasiveness. He's trying to take responsibility for the political failures of his country by relating them to his participation in an act of private betrayal. If America has abandoned thinking about long-range consequences and settled for acts of short-term self-interest, so has the speaker. If America has turned from the principles by which it defines itself, so has the speaker turned from his own principles. If America has lost its innocence so completely that it cannot mourn the loss, so the speaker is no longer "brave or lonely or free enough" to probe the meaning of his infidelity. "Lonely" is an important word here because it suggests that what seems an act of impulsive self-assertion, a brave disdaining of convention, is in fact a rejection of autonomy, a yielding to the values of the time rather than following one's better impulse. The comedy of the setting for this "patriotic kiss," the zoo parking lot, with its "orchestra of screaming birds" and "smell of elephant manure," helps underscore the absence of any real heroism in the lovers' "crossing over the border / of what [they] were supposed to do." The poem offers a negative formulation of Emerson's conviction that the state of society depends on the individual, that amendment of the social order begins with amendment of the self, a self disciplined enough to resist the pull to conformity. The dependence of the public on the private is richly suggested by the concluding simile, the comparing of the loss of personal principle to the blinking out of the streetlights of an imagined town. This town is the private embodiment of a public order that the speaker can no longer imagine, now that he knows himself unable to inhabit it.

Once writers begin to think of political life not as something determined by inaccessible governments but as shaped, at least in part, by the daily actions of ordinary citizens, they can view their own local acts of the imagination as relevant to the shaping of a political order. This relevance is likely to lie not in any immediate application of private insight to public policy but in the enacting of certain habits of concern that enlarge our notion of membership in the local community, a reaching out to include persons at the margin of the poet's usual focus. The imagination involved here is the faculty of moral sympathy described by Shelley, the chief means by which we understand the hidden life of others. In America we would probably consider Whitman our most important model for a sympathy of this kind. The speaker in a poem like "Song of Myself," disdaining the traditional hierarchies of polite society, identifies with everyone he encounters, regardless of vocation and social station; and this expression of empathy has the largest social implications. Whitman's ideal America is a country held together not by law or custom but by a network of imaginative filaments thrown out by autonomous individuals who want to include as many people as they can in their own acts of self-definition. Though at times we may wonder if Whitman's poet makes the act of empathy look too easy, giving too little attention to the resistance that has to be overcome for empathy to be successful, the model that he offers, of a self rich in proportion to its ability to include others, is still a vital one.

A great many of the most interesting poets today are engaged in this process of enlarging the local, poets who may not think of themselves as political writers but whose efforts at inclusiveness, however modest, have clear social implications. Consider Mark Halliday's "Fox Point Health Clinic, 1974," which not only enacts this process but relates it to shifting notions of the function of poetry:

In the waiting room this black woman maybe fifty sits down
right beside me. Whiskey breath; pocked face.
She looks over my shoulder at my notebook
where I've been writing about Bjorn Borg in a poem
whose point is that I should never cease
striving in life.
"That's beautiful."
A minute later: "I don't see too good."
A minute later: "I think I'm dying."
So I have to really look at her.
The Portuguese women waiting for the doctor don't seem to notice,
they murmur placidly.
My woman's eyes are round and dark.
I say "I certainly hope not."

She says "I'm all gone inside. Nothing but bones and ribs.
I've got three children.
My older son lives in Gardenia California.
My other son I don't know.
My daughter she'll be eighteen she goes to Saint Patrick's."
Her eyes ask me to figure what all this adds up to—
as if it's a technical puzzle and I'm the expert.
I nod, and look down.
She leans on me. "Every night I pray to God."
She clutches my hand and keeps it. "I'm gonna
tell you something. Love is beautiful."
I nod. "Black is beautiful too" she says.
I nod. She says, "I'm not black, I'm only teasing brown."
I make my eyes look into her eyes—best I can do;
if she's teasing it's a dark shade of teasing.

"I won't bug you anymore." She rises slowly
and soberly walks out. The Portuguese women shake their heads
as if they've seen my black woman do all this before.
I have a sore throat, I wish they would vanish, simply
vanish. But they don't; and gradually I work back toward
Bjorn Borg whose clarity and dedication have seemed so
fine, so pure, so white.[6]

Two very different poems are contrasted here, the poem that the
speaker is writing about Bjorn Borg, and the poem we have before us,
the speaker's description of how this project gets derailed by the in-
trusive black woman at the health clinic. The poem to Borg is essentially solipsistic, a piece of adolescent earnestness that uses Borg as a
private model for the speaker's own "striving in life." The story of the
black woman's intrusion involves the incursion into the private realm
of all the messy disorder of the world itself. Unlike the poem about
Borg, it seems to lead nowhere, to have no clear "point." The speaker

doesn't quite know what to make of his experience. Though he's distant enough from himself to see the interruption in comic terms, his return to the other poem at the end suggests that he does not see what the reader sees, that his direct reporting of the scene at the clinic is far more interesting than his treatment of Borg as a heroic ideal, even though the black woman, high on whiskey, offers no inspirational example and can't make any sense of the random facts of her own life. Instead of nuggets of wisdom, she leaves him only with a bromide about love, a political slogan, and a bit of private self-delusion. Yet the closing lines do suggest that the speaker is not going to be satisfied with the poem he returns to. Borg's "clarity and dedication" may have seemed "fine" and "pure" before, but the speaker would never have called them "white" until this moment, a term that suggests a new awareness of something small and provincial about his hero worship. He's left out too much experience. His use of the term "sober" to describe the black woman's exit suggests as well that he may be capable of seeing her as possessing real dignity. At least she knows how to draw the line between her own need for connection and the right of others not to be bothered. But the poem is nicely open about the exact state of the speaker's tolerance. What, for example, is the source of his anger at the Portuguese women? Is he angry because they are ahead of him in line when his sore throat calls for immediate attention, or because they fail to see what he has seen about the dignity of the black woman, or because he dimly perceives their narrowness in himself? In any case, his adolescent wish that they would "simply vanish" suggests that he still thinks of a community based on exclusion, not inclusion, and has a long way to travel before he can think of "dedication" and "striving" in social terms.

Halliday's "Fox Point Health Clinic" is a modest, comic poem without grand anger or bitterness. It does not take on the political establishment or suggest the poet's complicity in any large failure of America. Still it does present the poet with an important social role.

The health clinic may be only a health clinic, and the people in the waiting room only a random assortment of the sick; but society as a whole may be composed in good part by a network of such accidental groupings. And the poet, if he chooses to enter the world, may work to see the grouping as a potential community rather than as a collection of isolated individuals. This effort involves an act of sympathetic attention that the young poet resists and the writer of the poem before us manages to achieve. No amount of sensitivity will turn the black woman into a moral exemplar, like Wordsworth's leech-gatherer, who can help transform the listener in a radical way; but the poet's movement from isolation to engagement may be change enough. It suggests that the people in the health clinic don't have to be as separate as they seem to be, that the young poet, the black woman, the Portuguese women, and even Bjorn Borg may be part of a single story. Without any grand myth of discovering an *unum ex pluribus*, Halliday's poem, like others discussed here, provides a useful model for political involvement because it works away from exclusive definitions of the *polis* toward a critical engagement that enlarges our notion of how community should be defined.

CHAPTER FIVE

Midcourse Corrections

As I mentioned in the introduction, one of the objections made by skeptical critics against the speaker-centered view of poetry I am supporting here is that it presumes a self that it is unified when in fact, they contend, the self is a loose association of shifting qualities. This objection, I argued, presumes wrongly that the unified self necessary for a coherent speaker must be monolithic. Speaker-centered poetry may just as easily presume a self at odds with itself, the kind of self that Yeats is referring to when he asserts that his ghostly instructors "identify consciousness with conflict." [1] In the first chapter I discussed such poems of inner conflict in dealing with one of the ways the virtue of discrimination is dramatized in a speaker, and singled out in particular the post-Romantic poem of psychic narrative in which the speaker moves from one position to another, from confusion, say, to clarity, during the course of the poem. In this chapter I want to extend my argument by looking at more radical versions of this kind of poem, radical enough to suggest that in the course of the poem the speaker changes his notion of the kind of poem he is writing. Such a shift in genre may also suggest an answer to those who contend that the self, whether unified or not, is not free, for it grants the speaker the distance necessary for the kind of significant self-correction that freedom requires.

Though skeptics might argue that the poem of change is only one more rhetorical convention, the process that it enacts is in fact true to the process of revision by which most poems get written, a process that involves an openness to discovery, to the possibility that in the course of moving from first draft to final draft the point of view of a poem may undergo a radical change as the deeper implications of the subject slowly become clear. Often the last stages of revision involve removing the remnants of the original conception that are no longer adequate to the material. In a poem that places its shift of position in the foreground, the writer may be regarded as deliberately including his early versions in his final one, keeping a record of how he abandoned his initial stance as he moved toward an unanticipated conclusion. Such poems risk losing their energy by falling into discontinuous parts, but when they are successful they are particularly persuasive. They make their readers feel that their speakers' final positions are not preconceived pronouncements but something they discover despite themselves by following out the unforeseen implications of their material. Their initial schemes prove too small for the experience they want to understand and must in the interest of truth be expanded or discarded. To emphasize the fact that the single speaker need not be confined to a single perspective, that the sharply defined self may still be self-critical, fluid, and flexible, I want to focus here on a few poems that employ the midcourse correction as their organizing principle.

Three of the four poems I've chosen were written in the last thirty years, for the shifting poem is a particularly common form today, partly because our poets tend to work with liberal notions of poetic unity, and partly because they are reluctant to claim any special access to insight, regarding their statements as partial and provisional, not as exhaustive and final. But before I turn to these examples, I want to make the point that such poems may be found in any period when traditional categories of writing seem inadequate to the subjects that

poets feel compelled to explore. It's no accident that the shifting structure comes into its own in English poetry at the end of the eighteenth
century, when the classical genres seemed too public and outward to
deal with new psychological concerns and too rigid to deal with a new
conception of the self as developing over time, slowly discovering its
particular purposes under the pressure of experience. The neoclassi-
cal genres rejected by the Romantics were themselves ossified forms
of genres that Roman poets originated in an attempt to recast Greek
models to the needs of a new social order, an order that diminished
the ordinary citizen's involvement in public life and encouraged a
great expansion of private concerns. The new forms tended to allow
more room for the expression of personal differences, to value pe-
culiarities and inconsistencies as an essential part of human nature.
Horace may come first to mind in this regard, his readiness to present
himself as full of contradictions. And it might be useful, before turning to contemporary poems, to pause and look at one of his odes as
an example of a poem that changes its mind as it goes along, if only
to remind ourselves that in using the form today poets are not so
much inventing a new structure as adding their modifications to a
long tradition of resistance to strict notions of consistency.

Horace's ode on Octavian's victory over Cleopatra fits what I call a
poem of shifting direction because it seems to begin as a joyous public
celebration of the triumph of the imperial order and ends in private
brooding over the heroic death of Cleopatra:

> Now we must drink, my comrades,
> Now with free steps we must strike the earth,
> Now adorn the couch of the gods
> With Salian banquets.
>
> It would have been wrong before now
> To bring out the Caecuban wine from the ancient storerooms

As long as the crazed queen was plotting the downfall
Of our temple of Jupiter and the end of order,

She with her polluted crowd of men disfigured
By vices, unrestrained in her hopes
And drunk with good fortune.
But her fury slackened

When scarcely one of her ships escaped the flames.
And her mind, unsettled by the wine of Egypt,
Was forced to turn to its true terrors
When Caesar, as she fled from Italy,

Pursued her with his galleys. Just as a hawk
Chases a gentle dove, or a swift hunter
Stalks a hare on the plains of snowy Thessaly,
So Caesar followed, eager to put in chain

The deadly monster. But she, seeking a nobler way
To die, neither was frightened, as women are,
By the sword nor made her escape
In a swift ship to hidden shores.

With a face serene she dared to see her palace
Lying in ruins. And, with a stout heart,
She fondled deadly snakes, eager to take
Black venom into her body.

Having resolved on death, she grew more fierce,
Hating, surely, the thought of being borne off,
Deprived of her royal place, on enemy galleys,
For a proud triumph. A woman not to be humbled.[2]

The first four stanzas give expression to the poet's joyful relief that
he believes all true Romans must share at the death of a dangerous

enemy. The joy is especially intense because the enemy is presented as the demonic opposite of all that Rome stands for. Egyptian vice and fury have been vanquished by Roman probity and order. The poet underscores his identification with Roman decorum by insisting on the propriety of the celebration he calls for. What would have been out of place before the victory is now required by the occasion. The singing and dancing are not merely a natural release but a proper expression of gratitude to the gods that have protected Rome, and they are formally opposed to Cleopatra's drunken faith in fickle Fortuna. But in the last half of the poem, as the poet goes on to tell the story of Octavian's victory, the official dichotomies give way to a more personal response to Cleopatra's defeat and death. Though the description of her flight officially labels the queen as a "deadly monster" (*fatale monstrum*), it unofficially presents her as a pathetic victim, a gentle dove pursued by a hawk, a hare pursued by a hunter. These metaphors from the poet's sympathetic imagination have the effect of making the imperial terms sound crudely inappropriate. And sympathy triumphs in the conclusion as the poet openly admires Cleopatra for her resolute courage in facing death, her overcoming of fears natural to her situation and sex. The poet who began by rejoicing in the triumph of Rome over Egypt as the triumph of virtue over vice now praises Cleopatra for spoiling the final triumph of Octavian. The wild Egyptian escapes Roman humiliation by exercising the kind of proud determination typical of the Roman hero.

It would be a mistake, I think, to interpret the shift of subject and attitude enacted in the poem in subversive terms as an indirect attack on Roman ideals, in which the poet ironically pretends to civic feelings in order to reveal their falseness. One of the striking things about the poem is that whatever qualification it offers of traditional patriotism is made within the terms of Roman culture, not outside them. Praising an enemy of Rome for acting in ways a Roman audience can admire does not so much undermine Roman values as attempt to expand them, to redefine in larger ways what being a Roman means. The best justification for the freedom from disorder won by the Roman imperium, the poem implies, will be its providing a safe haven for the exercise of a citizen's individual sympathies, even when this exercise means doing justice to those whom the state cannot afford to tolerate. In enacting this kind of liberal sympathy, Horace is doing here something analogous to what Virgil does in the *Aeneid* when he allows his narrator to feel far more sympathy with the victims of Rome's founders than his hero can allow himself, sympathizing with Dido as Aeneas hardens himself against her, admiring the pastoral and heroic qualities of Latinus's kingdom that will not survive the triumph of Roman order. Like Virgil's narrator, Horace's speaker, not Octavian or Cleopatra, embodies the highest values of the poem.

Horace's expression of a more liberal model for Roman sympathies involves a wish to liberalize aesthetic attitudes as well, for it joins together two different kinds of poetry, public celebration and private musing, that were traditionally confined to two separate genres. The first part of the poem recalls Pindar's celebration of aristocratic contest and ceremonial reworkings of myth, and in its confident appeal to the poet's comrades *(sodales)* suggests that the poet sees himself as a master of ceremonies at a public ritual. But how many of his comrades does he presume are still listening when he turns to admire Cleopatra's shaping of her own death? Somewhere between the beginning and the end, the audience may have drifted away. The poet may consider himself lucky to be left with the single listener who is typically addressed in the *Odes,* the friend with whom the poet shares his observations on what promotes and undermines human happiness. What lies behind Horace's avoidance of the public, laudatory poem seems in part an Epicurean skepticism about the relation between public success and inner peace. The public realm for Horace, for whom the life of the Greek *polis* or the old Roman Republic is no longer available, is not the sphere in which character is likely to be fully defined or expressed. Its standards of virtue and happiness tend to be superficial. The poet's own attraction to the city of Rome, freely admitted in the *Satires,* is seen for the most part as an attraction for surfaces, not substance, while his Sabine farm comes to represent not merely a retreat from the pressures of town life but the home of the inner man, of that part of the self that lies deeper than the role assigned him as a citizen. In the ode on Cleopatra, Horace manages to enlarge the notion of citizen in a way that makes the development of private sensibility a crucial ingredient.

Though in harmony with the *Odes* in general in its questioning of official attitudes, the ode on Cleopatra is atypical in its structure, in its risking disunity by juxtaposing public and private attitudes toward the same subject. Today we may have an easier time appreciating the poem than did Horace's contemporaries, accustomed as we are to much looser notions of poetic unity; and we might be tempted to regard it as an ancestor of the kind of poem in which the poet adopts a number of perspectives with which he may only provisionally identify. But Horace's two views of Cleopatra do not lead to Stevens's five views of November off Tehuantepec. His ode does not attempt to hold its different attitudes in a playful, timeless suspension but to move from one to the other, and in doing so it presumes a more stable notion of the speaking self and its commitments. Yet in its divided structure it reminds us that a single-voiced speaker, ancient or modern, need not be rigid and monolithic. Rather than defend entrenched positions, he may instead choose to explore shifting concerns. In this respect the ode can be seen as an ancestor of a mode of contemporary poetry more common than Stevens's relativistic juxtapositions. The three well-known poems I've chosen as representative of the midcourse correction—Lowell's "For the Union Dead," Bishop's "At the Fishhouses," and C. K. Williams's "From My

Window"—are alike in enacting changes that may not be immediately apparent but which in fact involve shifts of perspective not only of subject or mood but of the kind of poem we are reading, of genre.

The speaker's change of direction is perhaps least obvious in "For the Union Dead," which may leave the reader with the impression of single-minded outrage at the cultural decay of midcentury America. But much of the poem's power comes from its discovering its real purpose only after trial and error. The first five stanzas have little to do with the subject announced in the title. They are more personal than public, and deal with the poet's feelings of separation from nature, not with the relation of American society to its political past:

> The old South Boston Aquarium stands
> in a Sahara of snow now. Its broken windows are boarded.
> The bronze weathervane cod has lost half its scales.
> The airy tanks are dry.
>
> Once my nose crawled like a snail on the glass;
> my hand tingled
> to burst the bubbles
> drifting from the noses of the cowed, compliant fish.
>
> My hand draws back. I often sigh still
> for the dark downward and vegetating kingdom
> of the fish and reptile. One morning last March,
> I pressed against the new barbed and galvanized
>
> fence on the Boston Common. Behind their cage,
> yellow dinosaur steamshovels were grunting
> as they cropped up tons of mush and grass
> to gouge their underworld garage.

Parking spaces luxuriate like civic
sandpiles in the heart of Boston.
A girdle of orange, Puritan–pumpkin colored girders
braces the tingling Statehouse[.][3]

The abandoned aquarium in South Boston that stirs the poet's recollections isn't presented as a symbol of the city's decline—for all we
know the city had good reasons to abandon it and has built a better
one elsewhere—but more as a reservoir of personal associations with
the poet's boyhood. Why the boy is fascinated by the "cowed, compliant fish" is left unclear, but we presume he sees aspects of their
passive condition within himself. His wish to break their bubbles can
be read as a protest against the kinds of civilized restraints he finds
himself having to bear. Yet the snail-like crawling of his nose on the
glass suggests that the likelihood of his own revolt is small. And the
child proves father of the man. The speaker is even less able as an
adult to connect with nature in a positive way. His elegiac "sigh" for
the "dark, downward, and vegetating kingdom / of the fish and rep-
tile" is more of a regressive fantasy of self-extinction than a hope for
real connection, a fantasy that is mocked by the poet even as he utters
it. But besides sighing, no options are considered available. Even the
cowed, compliant fish are gone from Boston, leaving in their place
grotesque mechanical parodies of nature like the "yellow dinosaur
steamshovels" digging a garage under the Common. The poet's alienation seems total, an aesthetic alienation more than a moral one, and
taken with his emotional passivity and his self-critical irony, it helps
define the speaker as a descendant of Eliot's Prufrock, a little less self-
conscious and self-justifying but equally unable to confront the world
he lives in.

Unless we can sense the limitations of the passive, ironic voice of
the speaker in these opening five stanzas, we are likely to miss the
striking transformation that takes place in the next five stanzas, where

the poet discovers his true subject, not the estrangement of the city
from nature but its estrangement from the best ideals of its own culture, those commemorated by the statue of Colonel Shaw leading his
colored troops into battle:

[A girdle of orange, Puritan–pumpkin colored girders
braces the tingling Statehouse,]

shaking over the excavations, as it faces Colonel Shaw
and his bell-cheeked Negro infantry
on St. Gaudens' shaking Civil War relief,
propped by a plank splint against the garage's earthquake.

Two months after marching through Boston,
half the regiment was dead;
at the dedication,
William James could almost hear the bronze Negroes breathe.

Their monument sticks like a fishbone
in the city's throat.
Its Colonel is as lean
as a compass-needle.

He has an angry wrenlike vigilance,
a greyhound's gentle tautness;
he seems to wince at pleasure,
and suffocate for privacy.

He is out of bounds now. He rejoices in man's lovely,
peculiar power to choose life and die—
when he leads his black soldiers to death,
he cannot bend his back.

The sleight of hand here that shifts the focus of the poem from nature
to culture is done so casually that we may miss the shift in tone that

accompanies it. The theme seems to find the poet, rather than the poet finding his theme. The decay of the aquarium has led him by contrast to think of the building he saw last March on the Boston Common, and the description of the statehouse leads by mere physical contiguity to the statue, which the poet then seems to seize on as a way to move from one mode of discourse to another, from ironic complaint to direct attack. This movement seems much less inevitable than the movement made by Horace's poet from triumph to pity, but the change is just as radical. If the poet has participated in the estrangement of the city from nature, he refuses to participate in its estrangement from its own past. He knows what the statue was intended to commemorate and feels keenly how the idealism that led Shaw to his death has been abandoned by a city indifferent to any but commercial values. The deeper emotional engagement of the speaker's imagination, and the power that accompanies it, is signaled in part by his newfound ability to make use of images from nature to help define cultural values. The realm of nature, toward which he can muster only self-mocking sighing in the first five stanzas, now becomes available to him as a resource for figures to define Shaw's moral superiority. The "fishbone" monument that the city can't swallow, the soldier's "wrenlike vigilance" and greyhound's "tautness" help define Shaw not as the product of a culture but as a model for the culture, outside its bounds in asserting the particularly human "power to choose life and die."

The shift of subject and attitude from that of the first five stanzas to that of the second constitutes a shift of genre, a turn from a private poem that is elegiac in tone to a public poem that is essentially satiric. And if Lowell's self-mocking lament has no single model behind it, the satire seems to be directly inspired by Juvenal. Just as Juvenal regards the corruption of imperial Rome as a betrayal of the best ideals of the Republic, so the speaker of Lowell's poem regards contemporary Boston as a betrayal of the heroic possibilities Shaw embodies. But Lowell's speaker is more aware than Juvenal's of the dangers of idealizing historical epochs. He does not want his penchant for trying to escape the present, displayed in personal terms in the opening of the poem, to take political form. He knows that rather than withdrawing into a past that is safely remote he needs to use the past to illuminate the problems of the moment. This is the issue he explores in the next five stanzas:

> On a thousand small town New England greens,
> the old white churches hold their air
> of sparse, sincere rebellion; frayed flags
> quilt the graveyards of the Grand Army of the Republic.

> The stone statues of the abstract Union Soldier
> grow slimmer and younger each year—
> wasp-waisted, they doze over muskets
> and muse through their sideburns . . .

> Shaw's father wanted no monument
> except the ditch,
> where his son's body was thrown
> and lost with his "niggers."

> The ditch is nearer.
> There are no statues for the last war here;
> on Boylston Street, a commercial photograph
> shows Hiroshima boiling

> over a Mosler Safe, the "Rock of Ages"
> that survived the blast. Space is nearer.
> When I crouch to my television set,
> the drained faces of Negro school-children rise like balloons.

The poet is not alone in appreciating the values that the statue embodies. At least in the small New England villages citizens make a genuine effort to keep the past alive, but their collective memory seems to grow increasingly removed from the bloody issues of the Civil War, so that the memorials grow irrelevant to the life of the moment. The danger of divorcing heroism from the ugliness of its context is presumably what prompts Shaw's father to think of the pit where Shaw and his men are buried as the best monument, a monument that would prevent the horrors of war from being forgotten. The kind of failure of historical memory that the wish anticipates is in fact borne out in contemporary Boston, where the men who died in even more brutal and more recent wars receive no monument and America's most indiscriminate wartime killing, the bombing of Hiroshima, is present only as an image in an advertisement for Mosler safes. In such a society all that the poet can do is record the triumph of everything that Shaw and his memorial try to resist. Crouched in front of the images of Negro children, he is a witness to the fact that the Civil War has yet to be won, that the slaves Shaw fought to free are still not citizens.

In his lack of power here, the poet may remind us of the speaker in the first part of the poem, and the image of the balloonlike faces of the children seems to recall the bubbles of the caged fish that fascinated the speaker when he was a boy. But the differences are more important than the likenesses. The fish in the glass case represent a pathetic attempt of the culture to maintain a connection with nature, but the faces on the television screen represent the culture's refusal to regard its own children as its members. The speaker in the first part of the poem daydreams of leaving behind a culture he can't connect to. The speaker of the last part builds in his satire a cultural monument that places idealism about a better order in the midst of the "pit" that denies it. At the end of the poem, the poet is as isolated as he was at the beginning, but now the isolation is not that of someone too delicate for the modern, industrial world but rather the kind that Juvenal enacts in his satires, that of a moral man who harbors no illusions about his power to arrest his society's decline. The only companion for Lowell's poet at the end is the statue of Shaw itself, which seems to be endowed in the penultimate stanza with the power to feel its own irrelevance:

> Colonel Shaw
> is riding on his bubble,
> he waits
> for the blesséd break.

Tired of riding the bubble of hope that his sacrifice might one day be embodied in social change, Shaw is ready to be released from the barren present. All that the speaker can do is remind himself what the statue should mean, to get beyond the idealizing of the past to a deeper awareness of beleaguered values, and to scorn a world that can't respond to them. In this project the poem is successful. It may be no more effective in correcting contemporary America than Juvenal's satire is in correcting Rome, but it does finally express the poet's power to name and condemn the tawdriness around him:

> The Aquarium is gone. Everywhere,
> giant finned cars nose forward like fish;
> a savage servility
> slides by on grease.

Against the savage servility of the culture, the poet, who begins his poem in nostalgic drift, affirms the force of savage indignation. And the power of his summation is underscored by the final use he makes of images from nature. The fish that he has associated in the opening with his own psychological passivity are now used as figures for the moral servility of the culture as a whole. Even as the poet describes the triumph of the less than human, his language enacts his authority to uphold countervailing human values.

"For the Union Dead" reverses the plot of Horace's ode by moving from the private realm to the public rather than from the public to the private. In both cases, however, the shift involves a critique of the social order, Horace's implied by his expansion of sympathy from Roman winners to foreign losers, Lowell's made directly as he attacks a society that has forgotten its ideals. The third poem I want to look at, Elizabeth Bishop's "At the Fishhouses," also involves a critique of the social order, but the terms are different. The society in question is a small fishing village on the Atlantic coast of Canada, which is presented as representative not of contemporary culture, whether imperial or democratic, but of civilization in general, here defined in the most primary terms as a settlement devoted to the hard winning of a living from nature. The shift of perspective that occurs in the poem does not entail a moral critique of the social order but rather a recognition of the limits of human power to impose shape on the world. Still the shift is equally significant, and involves an important redefinition of the poet's perspective. Here is the first section of the poem, which presents a reverential attitude to hard-won cultural achievement:

> Although it is a cold evening,
> down by one of the fishhouses
> an old man sits netting,
> his net, in the gloaming almost invisible,
> a dark purple-brown,
> and his shuttle worn and polished.
> The air smells so strong of codfish
> it makes one's nose run and one's eyes water.
> The five fishhouses have steeply peaked roofs

and narrow, cleated gangplanks slant up
to storerooms in the gables
for the wheelbarrows to be pushed up and down on.
All is silver: the heavy surface of the sea,
swelling slowly as if considering spilling over,
is opaque, but the silver of the benches,
the lobster pots, and masts, scattered
among the wild jagged rocks,
is of an apparent translucence
like the small old buildings with an emerald moss
growing on their shoreward walls.
The big fish tubs are completely lined
with layers of beautiful herring scales
and the wheelbarrows are similarly plastered
with creamy iridescent coats of mail,
with small iridescent flies crawling on them.
Up on the little slope behind the houses,
set in the sparse bright sprinkle of grass,
is an ancient wooden capstan,
cracked, with two long bleached handles
and some melancholy stains, like dried blood,
where the ironwork has rusted.
The old man accepts a Lucky Strike.
He was a friend of my grandfather.
We talk of the decline in the population
and of codfish and herring
while he waits for a herring boat to come in.
There are sequins on his vest and on his thumb.
He has scraped the scales, the principal beauty,
from unnumbered fish with that black old knife,
the blade of which is almost worn away.[4]

This opening section summons up the life of a small fishing village through an objective description of one particular visit that the poet makes to the fishhouses on the beach where the catch is stored. Instead of direct commentary on the value and meaning of the scene, the poet seems content to record the details before her as carefully as possible. That she has chosen a cold evening suggests that the scene provides her with more than the usual pleasures of the picturesque, but her sensitivity to the smell of the codfish also suggests that the scene is not one she lives in, and the way she moves from the fisherman to an itemizing of the materials of the trade—wheelbarrows, fishhouses, fish tubs, and capstan—suggests she is more interested in being true to her overall impressions, which are still novel for her, than in pushing for a revelation of meaning below the surface. What seems to charge the details she chooses is that they all show long wear. They are rubbed, smoothed, stained, and worn away over many years of use in the catching and handling of fish. Without any obvious aesthetic quality in themselves, they possess the kind of endearing homeliness that comes from long service in a difficult human enterprise. In this sense they stand for the simple way of life found in the village, and the final item in the series, the worn knife of the fisherman, overtly connects the objects of the trade with the days of a particular human life. That we are to think of this life as ennobling, not as constricting or enervating, is established indirectly through the description of the fish scales that cover every item in the scene. Their silvery sheen is a literal fact as obvious to the visitor as the smell of codfish, but they have a figurative weight in giving a strange beauty to the lowly objects of the trade, suggesting that they take on some of the strange beauty of the sea itself. The section reaches its climax with the inclusion of the fisherman in this silvery covering. Though he is an ordinary man, who smokes Lucky Strikes and chats about the decline of the fishing fleet, in practicing his calling he covers himself with sequins that make him figuratively a character in a pageant, in a lofty ritual that lifts him out of the realm of the ordinary and gives him a peculiar dignity.

If the poem had ended with the focusing image of the worn knife, it would have been an effective though subdued appreciation of a traditional human practice, somewhat elegiac in tone because the life of the fishing village is threatened, but ultimately celebrating the values implied by its endurance. But the short second section suggests that the poet has not finished her brooding on the scene:

> Down at the water's edge, at the place
> where they haul up the boats, up the long ramp
> descending into the water, thin silver
> tree trunks are laid horizontally
> across the gray stones, down and down
> at intervals of four or five feet.

What more she wants to say about the scene is at first not clear. The lines seem like an afterthought, prosy and flatfooted, as if the speaker is merely trying to make her description exhaustive by adding facts about the ramp that leads under the water. They don't prepare the reader for the sudden shift of emphasis that opens the third section, which makes up the second half of the poem:

> Cold dark deep and absolutely clear,
> element bearable to no mortal,
> to fish and to seals.

The lines arrest us first because they involve a shift of subject, from the winning of a living from the sea to the immutable otherness of the sea, its indifference, even hostility, to human life. And this shift causes the reader to see the fishing life presented in the first half of the poem as threatened by more than the laws of economics that make fishing less profitable. The sea can never be civilized, never be made part of human order. And with this shift of theme goes an equally deep shift in the reader's sense of the kind of poem he is reading. Up to this point the poet has built her theme through carefully observed, objective details, but with these lines she boldly generalizes about the human condition. The speaker who was content to place herself in a historical context, the granddaughter of a fisherman visiting his haunts on a particular occasion, now claims to speak timeless truths that are valid always and everywhere. And this claim to authority is underscored tonally by a shift in the music of the poem, from the loose casual notes of the first half to the heavy stresses and formal inversions that belong to a style that claims a grander inspiration.

The radical nature of the shift in genre is underscored in the first half of the last section by the poet's difficulty in sustaining her darker vision. Twice she introduces the sea, and twice she falls back, not ready to face its stark foreignness.

> [Cold dark deep and absolutely clear,
> element bearable to no mortal,
> to fish and to seals] . . . One seal particularly
> I have seen here evening after evening.
> He was curious about me. He was interested in music;
> like me a believer in total immersion,
> so I used to sing him Baptist hymns.
> I also sang "A Mighty Fortress Is Our God."
> He stood up in the water and regarded me
> steadily, moving his head a little.
> Then he would disappear, then suddenly emerge
> almost in the same spot, with a sort of shrug
> as if it were against his better judgment.
> Cold dark deep and absolutely clear,
> the clear gray icy water . . . Back, behind us,
> the dignified tall firs begin.

Bluish, associating with their shadows,
a million Christmas trees stand
waiting for Christmas.

Turning away from the intimidating sea, she abandons the seal as a stranger of the deep for the comforting comical fancy of the seal as a willing student of Baptist hymns. She then turns back to make another attempt to confront the sea boldly and again breaks off, this time feeling the need to comfort herself with the presence of the land behind her, not at ease even then until she has domesticated the "dignified tall firs" into a "million Christmas trees . . . waiting for Christmas." What finally allows her to confront the sea without fear is not made clear, but when she does rise to the challenge her voice is particularly assertive.

[A million Christmas trees stand
waiting for Christmas.] The water seems suspended
above the rounded gray and blue-gray stones.
I have seen it over and over, the same sea, the same,
slightly, indifferently swinging above the stones,
icily free above the stones,
above the stones and then the world.
If you should dip your hand in,
your wrist would ache immediately,
your bones would begin to ache and your hand would burn
as if the water were a transmutation of fire
that feeds on stones and burns with a dark gray flame.
If you tasted it, it would first taste bitter,
then briny, then surely burn your tongue.

She has seen a vision of the sea as a power stronger than anything else in the world, human or natural, swinging "above the stones and then the world," and has returned to report what this vision implies about human limits, to tell us that contact with this power is painful and deadly. The poet who has shown us, in the first half of the poem, that she can do justice to the beauty of a society that wins its simple living from nature now insists on a radical division. But in her ability to articulate this vision with magisterial confidence as she challenges and instructs us, she takes upon herself a kind of prophetic power.

That power displays itself overtly in the concluding six lines by finding an analogue for the sea in the human world:

> It is like what we imagine knowledge to be:
> dark, salt, clear, moving, utterly free,
> drawn from the cold hard mouth
> of the world, derived from the rocky breasts
> forever, flowing and drawn, and since
> our knowledge is historical, flowing, and flown.

We cannot know the ocean, and yet the ocean is analogous to "what we imagine knowledge to be," harsh human knowledge drawn not from gentle mothers but from the "cold hard mouth" and "rocky breasts" of experience in the world. In using "we," not "you," here, the speaker encourages us to rise to her pitch of seeing. And in her final insight she converts the sea's constant shifting into a metaphor for the shifting nature of our own convictions. Looking back with this perspective at the first part of the poem, we may view the daily toil of the fishing village as an analogue for the daily struggle to wrest insight from experience, a struggle that is endless because any particular truth is "historical," suffering aging and death, and so in need of constant replacement.

The end of the poem makes clear that the voice of timeless truth gains its authority by acknowledging the temporal nature of experience, and this emphasis can be seen as a comment on the poem itself, on its temporal structure that dramatizes a shift from one perspective to another. The end reminds us that the poem of self-correction is possible only when the speaker is engaged in a process of discovery rather than in the atemporal pronouncement of static conclusions. It is no accident that this kind of poem becomes common with the historical approaches to understanding self and society that arose at the end of the eighteenth century, approaches that are fully expressed in English poetry in Wordsworth's narrative meditations and Coleridge's conversation poems. These poems, and the poems they influence most directly, tend to be more deliberately immersed in the flow of immediate impressions than are the poems of Lowell and Bishop discussed here, more quietly associative in their transitions and more of a piece in tone and style. But if their shifts are more muted, the distance they travel from beginning to end is sometimes as great. C. K. Williams's "From My Window" owes a great deal to this romantic tradition:

> Spring: the first morning when that one true block of sweet,
>   laminar, complex scent arrives
> from somewhere west and I keep coming to lean on the sill,
>   glorying in the end of the wretched winter.
> The scabby-barked sycamores ringing the empty lot across the
>   way are budded—I hadn't noticed—
> and the thick spikes of the unlikely urban crocuses have already
>   broken gritty soil.
> Up the street, some surveyors with tripods are waving each other
>   left and right the way they do.
> A girl in a gym suit jogged by a while ago, some kids passed,
>   playing hooky, I imagine,
> and now the paraplegic Vietnam vet who lives in a half-converted
>   warehouse down the block
> and the friend who stays with him and seems to help him out
>   come weaving toward me,
> their battered wheelchair lurching uncertainly from one edge of
>   the sidewalk to the other.

I know where they're going—to the "Legion": once, when I was
    putting something out, they stopped,
both drunk that time, too, both reeking—it wasn't ten o'clock—
    and we chatted for a bit.
I don't know how they stay alive—on benefits most likely. I
    wonder if they're lovers?
They don't look it. Right now, in fact, they look a wreck,
    careening haphazardly along,
contriving, as they reach beneath me, to dip a wheel from the curb
    so that the chair skewers, teeters,
tips, and they both tumble, the one slowly, almost gracefully
    sliding in stages from his seat,
his expression hardly marking it, the other staggering over him
    spinning heavily down,
to lie on the asphalt, his mouth working, his feet shoving weakly
    and fruitlessly against the curb.
In the storefront office on the corner, Reed and Son, Real Estate,
    have come to see the show.
Gazing through the golden letters of their name, they're not, at
    least, thank god, laughing.
Now the buddy, grabbing at a hydrant, gets himself erect and
    stands there for a moment, panting.
Now he has to lift the other one, who lies utterly still, a forearm
    shielding his eyes from the sun.
He hauls him partly upright then hefts him almost all the way into
    the chair but a dangling foot
catches a support-plate, jerking everything around so that he has
    to put him down,
set the chair to rights and hoist him again and as he does he jerks
    the grimy jeans right off him.
No drawers, shrunken, blotchy thighs: under the thick, white coils
    of belly blubber,

the poor, blunt pud, tiny, terrified, retracted, is almost invisible in
    the sparse genital hair,

then his friend pulls his pants up, he slumps wholly back as
    though he were, at last, to be let be,

and the friend leans against the cyclone fence, suddenly staring up
    at me as though he's known,

all along, that I was watching and I can't help wondering if he
    knows that in the winter, too,

I watched, the night he went out to the lot and walked, paced
    rather, almost ran, for how many hours.

It was snowing, the city in that holy silence, the last we have, when
    the storm takes hold,

and he was making patterns that I thought at first were circles then
    realized made a figure eight,

what must have been to him a perfect symmetry but which, from
    where I was, shivered, bent,

and lay on its side: a warped, unclear infinity, slowly, as the snow
    came faster, going out.

Over and over again, his head lowered to the task, he slogged the
    path he'd blazed,

but the race was lost, his prints were filling faster than he made
    them now and I looked away,

up across the skeletal trees to the tall center city buildings, some,
    though it was midnight,

with all their offices still gleaming, their scarlet warning-beacons
    signaling erratically

against the thickening flakes, their smoldering auras softening
    portions of the dim, milky sky.

In the morning, nothing: every trace of him effaced, all the field
    pure white,

its surface glittering, the dawn, glancing from its glaze, oblique,
    relentless, unadorned.[5]

The most obvious shift in the poem is from spring to winter, but the meaning of that seasonal change is dependent on the prior shift of subject in the first section from the sights and smells of spring outside the speaker's window to the appearance of two drunken veterans who stumble into the poet's field of vision and seize his attention. The poet chooses to accept what chance has brought him rather than exclude intrusions that violate his initial project, and so the mood of the poem shifts from exuberance to a more somber kind of witnessing. This change of subject and mood is not marked by any obvious shift in style. The poet is still the sympathetic describer, not a participant. He looks down on the scene below from a distance that allows him to describe its grotesque and even farcical qualities with a clear-eyed, unsentimental precision. But he pities the humiliating plight of the veterans as well, and is glad that the other spectators, who come to the window of their office to watch the show, just as he does, don't respond with derision.

The speaker's status as a sympathetic onlooker is disrupted, however, by the incident that brings about the second shift of the poem, in which the friend of the crippled veteran looks up to notice the poet observing him "as though he'd known all along that [the poet] was watching." The buddy's perspective, which seemed small compared to the poet's, ground-level and drunken as opposed to high and clear-eyed, suddenly expands to include the poet's within it. The buddy is both participant and removed observer who knows as well as the poet, if not better, the bleakness and grotesqueness of the drama he is enacting. The collapse of the poet's privileged distance is made clear in his recollection of the winter scene that ends the poem. Here the buddy, alone at night in the empty lot, performs a dance in the snow that expresses his own vision of the hopelessness of his own life, and by implication the hopelessness of the human condition. Whether his desires are finite or infinite, the tramping of a sign that is immediately obliterated acts out his own awareness of the absurdity of his wishes and the degree of his powerlessness. Introduced with his friend as part of a comic and pathetic interlude, he becomes by the end of the poem its hero, who deserves not only pity but awed appreciation. The change from spring to winter ultimately marks an important change of perspective that makes use of the traditional associations of spring with comedy and winter with tragedy, from looking down on the world with amused detachment to looking up.

Though the poet gets demoted in terms of his relation to the buddy, the ennobling of the buddy suggests that the poet is empowered as well, that he moves to a deeper level of empathy, and this empowerment is enacted overtly by his leaving observation for recollection. The poet initially identifies himself as an observer honest enough to witness what the world is really like, not merely what he hopes it will be like. But the poet of winter presents himself as someone who completes the present with his own memories. The full revelation of meaning requires a deeper effort of the imagination, even if the imagination is represented in its most basic form of making present what is absent, bringing before our eyes what is no longer available, making winter present in the midst of spring. Meaning is latent in the moment, but it requires the poet to make it actual. Only through the imagination can the figures before us be done full justice.

The expansion of the poet's role that is enacted in "From My Window" reminds us that the shift of position that lies at the center of all the poems we have examined is not felt as a self-cancellation, in which the text seems to undermine its own authority by the juxtaposing of contradictory positions. It dramatizes rather an act of self-correction in which the speaker moves from one position to another in an attempt to engage life more fully. The self presented in the poem is not frail or shifting, composed of a set of discontinuous attitudes. It develops in time, changing its perspective under the pressure of experience, exploring one position on the way toward adopting a counter-position that qualifies and contains the first. Skeptical postmoderns might want to argue that this gaining of larger insight is an illusion, that the final perspective is as partial as the initial one, equally influenced by the prevailing orthodoxies of the time, equally governed by the reigning vocabulary. But all the poems we've looked at suggest that even if the poets cannot step out of their times completely, different degrees of removal are available. They all enact changes in which the poet seems to step away from easy notions of community. The movement is evident in Horace's turning from celebrating Rome's victory to his sympathizing with Rome's enemy, in Lowell's changing from passive victim of his age to angry contemner, and in Bishop's shift from appreciating the beauty of communal struggle to her stark delimiting of human power. Even Williams's poet, while overcoming emotional distance from the scene, can be said to move away from harmony with the social order, from an easy, genial acceptance of urban variety that is promoted by the window perspective to a radical vision of human isolation and constriction.

Just as the poems resist contemporary skepticism about the poet's claim to authority, they resist a similar skepticism about the ability of traditional genres to move and enlighten. Genres need not be regarded as prescribing outmoded attitudes. They can be used as tools that poets feel free to adapt to the particular demands of their subject. As the example of Horace makes clear, the impulse to modify the tradition by combining genres is built into the tradition itself. Horace's shift from public ode to private elegy gives the backing of tradition to Lowell's shift from elegy to satire, Bishop's shift from imagistic encomium to prophetic pronouncement, and Williams's shift from a poem of spring to a poem of winter. As long as writers are open to many genres, not merely one, and are not reluctant to shift from one to another in order to say what needs to be said, this tradition, far from restricting their freedom, may help give shape to their concerns and free them from the pressures to succumb to the dominant provincialities of their times. If we want to throw fresh light on the world, we would do well to be pluralists as Horace was a pluralist, accepting as he did the different assumptions of different genres and practicing within one poem a free-spirited dialogue that welcomes revision. With that kind of openness, we should be able to discover the particular stories we want to tell.

CHAPTER SIX

Myth

⚜

POEMS like those discussed in the last chapter, in which the speaker seems to shift direction in a radical way, imply a speaker who is both modest and self-assured. He is modest to the extent that he is willing to suggest that his conclusions do not spring from his mind fully formed, that in the very act of articulating what he believes, he may find his notions mistaken, that he must grope toward meaning. And he is self-assured to the extent that he presumes his confusions and self-corrections are at least as interesting to the reader as his final pronouncements; that the process, wherever it ends, is representative of certain habits of mind with which the reader may easily identify. Without humility the speaker would not place the limitations of his initial state of mind so clearly in the foreground; without self-assertion he would not believe the shift worth telling about. But while these contrasting virtues are both embodied in this genre, humility is more obviously dramatized. The self-assuredness is only indirectly implied, in the presumption that all poetry is based on, that the ex-periences it deals with are representative, while the humility is placed in the foreground by the deliberate focusing on the need of the speaker to enlarge his initial perspective. In certain other kinds of poems, however, this emphasis is reversed, with the speaker's self-assertiveness given the central position as he emphasizes the significance of his subject. Poems that use myth are an obvious case in point, because they make the claim of having something to say that has archetypal significance. How to make such claims convincingly, without sounding as if one is claiming too much, is the chief rhetorical problem of the genre.

Poets who uses myth successfully need not, of course, believe that the myth referred to is true in any literal way, nor is the reader required to believe in such truth for the reference to be telling. "The woods of Arcady are dead," Yeats announces in the first line of the poem he chose to place at the beginning of his first book of poems, *Crossways,* but that announcement of loss of belief did not prevent him from using Greek myth in his poetry throughout his life, nor has it prevented more recent poets from returning to it even though they are far removed from the Romantic tradition of Yeats that venerated Greek culture. In a similar way Biblical stories keep appearing in poets who do not believe the Bible is divinely inspired, who may regard it as Emily Dickinson's speaker sometimes does, as only "an antique volume written by faded men." One reason for this persistence is that myth is an important source for the few stories that poets can count on their readers to know, stories that have been used by so many and for so long that they are part of the history of our culture, the source of many of its traditional examples of human behavior. Viewed in this secular way, the plots and characters of myth are like the plots and characters of fiction or drama that have become familiar to most readers. This equivalence allows Eliot's Prufrock, near the end of his song of frustrated love, to compare himself in turn to John the Baptist, Lazarus, Hamlet, and Odysseus, using this mixed group of figures to define himself in a way that is both concise and complex.

For Prufrock, of course, it is his difference from these fictive characters, not any similarity, that prompts the comparisons. Their high examples do not lead him to emulation, only to a self-mocking recognition of what he lacks. "The Love Song" has in fact served as a model for poets today who choose to use myth ironically, to define the limitations of our own times through a contrast with traditional heroes. Prufrock is "no prophet" like St. John, though he wishes he had a message like John's and the courage to deliver it; no dead man brought to life like Lazarus, though he's well aware that the city he lives in sorely needs a spiritual resurrection; and no Hamlet, who after hesitating for four acts is able in the last act to seize the moment. And unlike Odysseus he is unable to imagine, even in fantasy, the mermaids' thinking him worth tempting. In using myth in the service of satire, Eliot places his poem in the tradition of Pope and Swift, but his hero, unlike the knaves and fools of a poem like the *Dunciad,* is at least granted the dignity of seeing the discrepancies for himself. Though he may regard the distance between himself and his fictive models as unbridgeable, he does accept the values they embody as relevant for judging his life. And in the seriousness with which he applies the myths to himself he seems closer, despite his ironic stance, to the speaker of a first-person Romantic lyric than he does to the typical speaker in Augustan satire. Even when Pope writes satire in the first person, he usually follows the lead of Horace and Juvenal in avoiding mythic material. Juvenal, it should be remembered, opens his book of satires with an attack on irrelevant mythological exercises that ignore the abuses of the times, poems that make the cave of Mars more familiar to the reader than his own house. In turning from public poems to poems of psychological exploration, the Romantics reinstate classical myth as an important source for archetypes of consciousness, and as a Romantic manqué Prufrock accepts the judgment implied by his failure to measure up to mythic models.

Though "The Love Song" provides one possible model for using myth today, it also shows the limits of its approach; for Prufrock's reliance on irony is presented as a symptom of his deepest problems, disengagement and passivity. If myth is to be used to enlarge one's sense of possibility rather than restrict it, the poet has to learn to leave irony behind. Eliot deals with this problem directly in *The Waste Land,* where much of the drama involves the effort of the multivoiced speaker to move from satiric contrasts to reenactments of mythic archetypes. He is not content with anatomizing the corpse of the modern world. He wants to revive the dead land, and myth helps him define not only what is missing but what in the present participates in a timeless pattern. So when the speaker presents himself as the lover of the "hyacinth girl," the passage from Wagner's *Tristan und Isolde* that he uses as a frame seems intended less to mock his failure to express himself than to suggest that this failure is a modern version of an age-old problem. Our lover has had a vision of both fullness and emptiness, has looked "into the heart of light, the silence," and the vision has left him speechless, "neither living nor dead." And though the trash-littered Thames of the modern world is a demythologized version of the river presented in Spenser's "Epithalamion," the lament of the Thames maidens is not so much a mockery of the river's plight as a reenactment in modern terms of the lament of the Rhine Maidens from Wagner's *Götterdämmerung;* for both sets of maidens have been despoiled, have lost their treasure and their meaning, and like the lovers can "connect nothing with nothing." The speaker of the poem has chosen mythic figures that do not mock him with their perfection so much as mirror in larger terms his own predicament. And this choice is particularly telling in the speaker's identifying himself with Tiresias. In the prophet from Greek tragedy he has found an analogue for insight like his own that does not seem to be of use to those around him, that lacks the power to transform and redeem. But if the name serves to emphasize his frustration, it also serves to give a mythic status to his own impotence, to suggest it is not merely a personal failure but a reenactment of a larger pattern.

Most poets who regularly use myth today would endorse Eliot's

shift from an ironic to a more engaged handling of his material because it opens poetry to a wider range of tones, from doubt to conviction, from distance to participation. But they also tend to favor techniques more direct than those of *The Waste Land,* less mediated by
the role-playing that makes Eiot's poem a kind of poetic drama. Often
they seem to favor first-person poems where the distance between
writer and speaker is small, far smaller than it is in a dramatic monologue like "Prufrock." And they often attempt this kind of statement
by concentrating on a single mythic strand rather than by the kind
of mixing of mythic sources practiced in *The Waste Land,* where the
speaker's frantic moving among eclectic materials—pagan, Hebrew,
Christian, and Buddhist—betrays the desperation of his search for
coherence. The crucial aesthetic challenge these poets face in enlarging the resonance of their poems through myth is to avoid claiming
too much importance for their assertions. This task is particularly
challenging in a skeptical period like ours that is wary of any claims
to special insight.

In the first-person poem the most common symptom of failure
in meeting this challenge is a speaker who sounds self-important.
Though I want to concentrate in this chapter on poetic success, it
might be useful to look first at an instance of this problem. Here is a
poem by Yehuda Amichai, a writer whose work I often admire, but
who seems to me in this case not to have used myth convincingly:

> *The Place Where I Have Not Been*
>
> The place where I have not been
> I shall never be.
> The place where I have been
> Is as though I have never been there. People stray
> Far from the places where they were born

And far from the words which were spoken
As if by their mouths
And still wide of the promise
Which they were promised.

And they eat standing and die sitting
And lying down they remember.
And what I shall never in the world return to
And look at, I am to love forever.
Only a stranger will return to my place. But I will set down
All these things once more, as Moses did,

After he smashed the first tablets.[1]

Not knowing Hebrew, I can't tell whether this translation is faithful to the original, or whether the original works because of the peculiar openness of the language to Biblical reference; but as I read it in English its conclusion seems unearned. The reader can appreciate the decorum involved in reserving the reference for the end, after the theme of loss has been established, but the analogy of the poet to Moses seems to claim too much. In what way are the poet's lines like the revelation that Moses receives on Mount Sinai and transcribes for the Hebrews? Not in their divine origins, surely, or in their announcing a set of laws that can guide a people's actions. For the poet's subject is the mutability of all human enterprise. One might argue that in linking the poet's work specifically with the second pair of tablets, as opposed to the ones that Moses broke in anger, the speaker wants to suggest that he too writes from a sense of disappointment of expectation; he too has hoped for more and must reconcile himself to defective materials. But the speaker's disappointment seems to spring less from a sharpened sense of man's moral weakness than from a sense of what it means to live in the world of time. If the "straying" that people do suggests their being distracted from their true purposes, that distraction is presented as part of the human condition, of living in a mutable, shifting world that places the past forever out of reach and forces us "to eat standing and die sitting." And from the beginning, the poet includes himself among those who are "wide of the promise / Which they were promised." The last line, then, seems oddly inappropriate, for the speaker we have seen has had to overcome no indignation like that of Moses at the infidelity of the Hebrews. He has had rather to recommit himself to love what he knows is governed by the law of mortality. As a result, his concluding claim to identity with Moses ends up sounding too much like a last-minute attempt to give heroic status to a decidedly unheroic definition of the poet's limitations. This misstep is particularly jarring because until the last two lines the poem is particularly sure-footed, moving gracefully and concisely from the speaker's own condition to that of mankind in general, endowing an abstract language with vividness by grounding the phases of life in movements of the body. The lesson here for the apprentice writer is that even masterful poets have to be on their guard when they're drawn to myth, vigilant against making claims that can't be supported by their material.

Among the great moderns, the poet who serves many contemporary poets as a model for the non-ironic use of myth is Yeats, who builds the importance of heroic models into his theory of psychic development, at least for the development of what he calls the "subjective" personality. Through the imposition of masks borrowed in part from myth, an aesthetic temperament prone to disperse its energies in quarrels with the world imposes on itself an austere, solitary, heroic discipline that makes a creative life possible. How Yeats manages to apply the theory to his own life without sounding as if he were making grandiose claims for significance can be seen clearly in the way he handles the theme in a simple lyric like "A Woman Homer Sung":

If any man drew near
When I was young,
I thought, 'He holds her dear,'
And shook with hate and fear.
But O! 'twas bitter wrong
If he could pass her by
With an indifferent eye.

Whereon I wrote and wrought,
And now, being grey,
I dream that I have brought
To such a pitch my thought
That coming time can say,
'He shadowed in a glass
What thing her body was.'

For she had fiery blood
When I was young,
And trod so sweetly proud
As 'twere upon a cloud,
A woman Homer sung,
That life and letters seem
But an heroic dream.[2]

If we remove the title and its one-line repetition, we have a poem that
seems to work well enough without mythical reference, clearly affirming the poet's efforts to do justice in his art to the beauty of the woman
he's loved. But the line adds a striking resonance to the whole by raising the stakes of the poet's assertions. He has not merely devoted himself to any beautiful woman but to the equal of Helen of Troy, and his
commitment to describing her reenacts Homer's commitment to his
heroine. How does Yeats get away with this seeming hyperbole? Partly
because, in contrast with Amichai's poem, the mythic analogy in his

poem focuses primarily on the glory of the speaker's beloved, not on the speaker himself. Moreover, Yeats has used the postponement of the analogy to the end to establish a speaker who can look with a critical distance on his own life. In the first stanza he laughs at the inconsistencies of the young lover who is both jealous of all who admire his lady and angry at all who fail to admire her. And in the second stanza, he gives up the role of lover for that of a gray-haired chronicler, writing not to please his lady but to give future readers a glimpse of her beauty, and modest enough about his abilities to admit that this glimpse will only be a shadow of the real thing. Once we have been given these signs of the poet's modesty, we are more likely to allow his grand comparison. Moreover, the last stanza, particularly the closing lines, suggests that the poet is objective not only about the limits of his powers but also about the limiting effect of his commitment on his own life. His love for his lady has turned his life into "an heroic dream," and if we place a stress on the noun rather than the adjective, a stress that the word "but" seems to support, we may conclude the poet finds that his sublimation of love into art has left his life dreamlike in the sense of unreal rather than merely rare and strange. For the reader prone to look for hidden negations that "deconstruct" the overt meaning of a text, this qualification might seem to cancel out all the apparent affirmation. Our would-be Homer, hoping to give his subject immortality, has ended up merely with dream art and dream life. But this reading would have to ignore the emphatic, assertive tone of the poem, which suggests that though the costs of the poet's commitment are real, the gains are real as well. He has celebrated in his art a woman who is worth celebrating, and this task has made his life heroic even if it has kept him from ordinary successes in the world. How can his choice be judged as a mistake when Homer himself made the same choice, devoting his art to a woman of similar fire?

If we limited ourselves to looking for poems that follow the model of "A Woman Homer Sung" in giving a mythic reading to one's life-long commitments, we might be hard pressed to see the influence of Yeats's handling of myth on contemporary poetry. Even in Yeats's own work such poems are not common, and they are much more difficult to write in unheroic times like ours when writers go in fear of taking themselves too seriously. We are more comfortable viewing our judgments as expressions of a personal perspective rather than objective acts of historical witnessing that preserve a true record for the benefit of "coming time." And yet a plain-speaking poet like Jack Gilbert, whose speaker tends to talk in a calm voice about personally observed particulars, comes close to Yeats at times in his use of elevating myth. Here is "Remembering My Wife":

> I see them in black and white as they wait,
> severely happy, in the sunlight of Thermopylae.
> As Iseult and Beatrice are always black and white.
> I imagine Helen in light, not hue. In my dreams,
> Nausicaa is blanched colorless by noon.
> And Botticelli's Simonetta comes as faint tints of air.
> Cleopatra is in color almost to the end.
> Like Linda's blondeness dyed by flowers and the sea.
> I loved that wash of color, but remember her
> mostly black and white. Marc Antony listening
> to Hercules abandoning him listened in the dark.
> In that finer time of day. In the essence, not the mode.[3]

For our purposes the central aesthetic question in this bold poem is whether the poet manages to insert his wife into a list of historical and mythological luminaries without sounding foolish. I want to argue that he does, in good part because he balances his bold juxtaposition with a quiet restraint that refrains from making the kind of direct assertion of equivalence that is made in Yeats's poem. Linda, it's worth noting, appears only after the poem seems to have defined itself as a precise, calm, and neutral description of the workings of the poet's imagination and memory on characters from myth and idealized history. It gives an objective description of the subjective fact that they appear in his mind as black and white rather than colored. And when Linda is introduced, she enters casually, as the poet tries to define for himself the shade of lightness in Cleopatra's coloration. Only in the next sentence do we learn that the same process of abstraction, from color to black and white, has occurred with Linda as well. And as far as we can tell, at this point in the poem, this process entails more loss than gain, with memory losing beloved details that keep her image distinct and individual. Only in the closing lines are we told that the poet believes this shift entails an intensification of insight, that in moving from color to black and white he moves not from bright reality to pale copy but from surface to depth, from shifting "mode" to changeless "essence." But even at this moment when his knowledge is validated, the poet leaves it to the reader to draw the kind of conclusions that Yeats insists on, that Linda possesses an archetypal resonance equal to that of the mythic women, that she inhabits not the ordinary world of prose but the world of heroic poetry.

The success of the poem's rhetoric is underscored when we realize that the poem shifts unobtrusively from subjective commentary about the workings of the poet's mind to a general statement about how all minds work. The speaker's mode of abstraction is not only true for him but constitutes a truer kind of seeing for everyone. To make this generalization convincing, the speaker deflects attention from himself at the crucial moment of affirmation, turning to the example of Antony, who also possesses the deeper knowledge of seeing "in the finer time of day" when color disappears. This move is risky because the poet, in using Antony as his stand-in, seems to be claiming for himself the same kind of heroic status he's claimed for his wife. But the association with Antony follows naturally from the poet's linking of Linda and Cleopatra, and the linkage is so dark in its implications that it can't be read as a symptom of grandiosity. Just as Antony's deeper seeing comes at the moment he recognizes that all is lost, that his protecting god has abandoned him, so the poet seems to view his deeper knowledge of Linda as arriving only with his losing her. He possesses insight about her essential being when he no longer possesses her in life. This darkening of tone is similar to the suggestion in Yeats's poem that the poet's commitments have rendered his life dreamlike, insubstantial as well as heroic. But as in Yeats's poem the loss to the speaker does not cancel out the gain. And for the reader the loss is crucial in winning credibility for the remarkable elevation of the poet's affirmations that results from the use of the mythic material. A private loss has been given a heroic resonance, imbued with an uncommon weight and dignity.

These poems by Yeats and Gilbert represent a conservative use of myth in that they view the figures of myth as partaking of a higher order of reality than common life, an order to which they try to gain access by a carefully managed assertion of equivalencies. But many poets today are uneasy with the veneration for myth that this approach implies. They find myth full of dubious and troubling assumptions about man's relations to divine powers, to nature, and to his fellow humans, and want to explore or expose these assumptions rather than to make contact with a timeless reality. In keeping a critical distance from the myths they use, these writers are not so much leaving tradition behind as working in an established counter-tradition in American poetry that goes back at least as far as Whitman and Dickinson. Whitman's celebration of man's boundless capacity to find the world within himself, especially clear in "Song of Myself," requires that traditional religion be revised by interpreting its external gods as disposable names for the limitless energies residing within the human psyche:

Magnifying and applying come I,
Outbidding at the start the old cautious hucksters,
Taking myself the exact dimensions of Jehovah,
Lithographing Kronos, Zeus his son, and Hercules his grandson,
Buying drafts of Osiris, Isis, Belus, Brahma, Buddha,
In my portfolio placing Manito loose, Allah on a leaf, the crucifix
   engraved.[4]

The old gods have now been outgrown: "They bore mites as for un-
fledg'd birds who have now to rise and sing for themselves." Needed
in the infancy of the human race to keep alive man's sense of the
divine, they must now be retired as we come to a recognition of our
own powers. For Dickinson, on the other hand, with her emphasis on
human limits, the god we approximate is Christ, and the story of his
suffering has to be reinterpreted in order to elevate man's divine capacity for tragedy:

   One Crucifixion is recorded—only—
   How many be
   Is not affirmed of Mathematics—
   Or History—

   One Calvary—exhibited to Stranger—
   As many be
   As persons—or Peninsulas—
   Gethsemane—

   Is but a Province—in the Being's Centre—
   Judea—
   For Journey—or Crusade's Achieving—
   Too near—

Our Lord—indeed—made Compound Witness—
And yet—
There's newer—nearer Crucifixion
Than That—[5]

In asserting that "Gethsemane is but a Province in the Being's Centre," the poem implies a critique of the orthodox Christian reading of
the Passion, which focuses on the unique nature of Christ's torment.
Here Christ on the cross is not a redeemer, only an image of the kind
of inner crucifixion that any human may have to undergo. But what
Christ loses in status we humans gain. We are all gods, and Jesus is
our brother, gods neither omnipotent nor immortal, to be sure, but
divine in our power to suffer deeply.

Contemporary poets who follow the lead of Dickinson and Whitman in criticizing traditional myth may often do so without attempting to elevate man. They may simply be trying to expose the way a
reliance on an unexamined myth may prevent an honest and open
response to the world. Consider Amy Gerstler's "Sirens":

I have a fish's tail, so I'm not qualified to love you.
But I do. Pale as an August sky, pale as flour milled
a thousand times, pale as the icebergs I have never seen,
and twice as numb—my skin is such a contrast to the rough
rocks I lie on, that from far away it looks like I'm a baby
riding a dinosaur. The turn of centuries or the turn
of a page means the same to me, little or nothing.
I have teeth in places you'd never suspect. Come. Kiss me
and die soon. I slap my tail in the shallows—which is to say
I appreciate nature. You see my sisters and me perched
on rocks and tiny islands here and there for miles:
untangling our hair with our fingers, eating seaweed.[6]

The speaker here may at first seem to be a modern version of the siren who tempts men to their doom, speaking for that part of woman that lies beyond history, dangerous to men who wish to make women wholly a part of culture. But the more we look at her boasts the more ironic they appear. Unlike the Sirens of myth, this speaker is in love with a particular man, the "you" she is addressing, an admission that suggests she is only an ordinary woman who is playing the role of siren. Why should she play the role if it leaves her "not qualified" to receive the love of the "you"? Apparently the role is not one she has willingly chosen but rather one that he has foisted upon her. Viewed by him as fundamentally different, she seems resigned to play the part of mermaid as well as she can, even though it forces her into melo-dramatic poses. In her stage makeup designed for the passing sailors, she is as "pale as the icebergs [she] has never seen," an impossible combination of tender innocence and colossal animality ("a baby rid-ing a dinosaur"), together with a witchlike sexual menace. Whatever she does, whatever signs of pleasure or exuberance, her gestures are read by the "you" as aligning her feelings with nature, not with the culture that he is a part of. Her concluding reference to hair and sea-weed may make us think of the concluding images of Prufrock, but the differences are more important than the similarities:

> We have lingered in the chambers of the sea
> By sea-girls wreathed with seaweed red and brown
> Till human voices wake us, and we drown.

Prufrock imagines himself as a man who has wasted his feelings on fantasies, who lacks the kind of heroic potency to confront in life the energies that the Sirens embody. But here the "you" has failed as a lover by transforming the speaker into a mermaid when she wants to be a human being. The reduction implied by the myth comes out comically in the image of the seaweed. Prufrock's mermaids *wind* seaweed in their hair. These mermaids *feed* on seaweed because they have become for the "you" wholly other, pure creatures of nature. By claiming ironically to fill all the fantasies of the "you," the speaker protests against the myth imposed on her, though her protest is also a recognition that because of her love she has been willing to succumb to the imposition. In this sense she is under a spell, a prisoner of enchantment, like the heroine of a fairy tale, but no hero is on his way to deliver her from her siren shape with a magic kiss. She has fallen in love in fact with the sorcerer himself, a sorcerer not aware of his sorcery, doomed to be trapped forever in his own magic projections.

Gerstler's poem uses the myth of the Sirens to give weight to the man's limited perspective, suggesting that the problems of the "you" are not simply the product of one person's psychology but a part of the bedrock of our culture. She can be said to revise the myth by providing a woman's view of a situation traditionally presented in male terms, showing how male fears trap both man and woman in false positions. The poem provides a good example of the way revision may involve a repudiation of a mythic perspective while still acknowledging its power. It may be contrasted with poems that revise myth without limiting its scope, that try to present contemporary versions of myth that validate the archetype rather than repudiate it. In this more affirmative mode the poet accepts the myth as offering a model of behavior still useful for evaluating the present but requiring modifications in order to do justice to the variety of contemporary reenactments. Here is Linda Gregg's contemporary version of the story of Orpheus and Eurydice, "Eurydice":

> I linger, knowing you are eager (having seen
> the strange world where I live)
> to return to your friends
> wearing the bells and singing the songs
> which are my mourning.

With the water in them, with their strange rhythms.
I know you will not take me back.
Will take me almost to the world,
but not out to house, color, leaves.
Not to the sacred world that is so easy
for you, my love.

Inside my mind and in my body is a darkness
which I am equal to, but my heart is not.
Yesterday you read the Troubadour poets
in the bathroom doorway
while I painted my eyes for the journey.
While I took tiredness away from my face,
you read of that singer in a garden
with the woman he swore to love forever.

You were always curious what love is like.
Wanted to meet me, not bring me home.
Now you whistle, putting together
the new words, learning the songs
to tell the others how far you traveled for me.
Singing of my desire to live.

Oh, if you knew what you do not know
I could be in the world remembering this.
I did not cry as much in the darkness
as I will when we part in the dimness
near the opening which is the way in for you
and was the way out for me, my love.[7]

Like the Orpheus of fable, the lover here has descended into the dark
world to which his beloved has been confined, with the ostensible
purpose of leading her back to the light; and like him he is doomed

to fail in the enterprise. But this Orpheus will fail not from forgetting, in a moment of concern, a prohibition to look behind him, but from abandoning his companion on the way. The lover may believe that his love is genuine, but he is less interested in bringing back the woman he pretends to love than in bringing back songs that describe his journey. Returning without his Eurydice will allow him to boast of his sacrifices and suffering without having to endure the prosaic burdens of commitment and loyalty. The implications of this revision of the myth are not immediately clear. If the poem consisted only of the first stanza, we might be justified in reading the poem as a critique of the myth's idealism, as revealing the harsher truth about human nature behind the official tragic version. But the homely details of the second stanza make clear that the poem is an attempt not to attack the myth but to use it to clarify an autobiographical episode. The speaker is a woman in the present moment, and her boyfriend, concerned more with assuming the poetic postures of love—like the troubadour poets he admires—than with actual loving, fails to measure up to a man of deeds like Orpheus. In using the myth as a model by which we can measure a present fall, the poem bears a kinship with "Prufrock," but the tone is very different from the self-mockery of Eliot's poem because it is presented from the woman's perspective, a woman who believes her fate rests in her lover's hands. Prufrock's lady, for all we know, would not welcome his advances even if he were bold enough to make them. But here we have a speaker who believes she could be saved from a kind of psychic burial by the hero's love and must come to terms with the fact that such love will not be granted.

One might expect that in comparing her love-loss to imprisonment in an underworld and her dream of love to a return from death to life, the speaker might run the risk of sounding melodramatic, as if she were trying to cover over a commonplace humiliation with a borrowed grandeur. But her tone of voice is so poised, so quiet in a situation that might be expected to call for complaint or challenge, that we never question her authority. Though she uses the second person, she does so more to suggest her attachment to the "you" than to indicate any literal appeal. She is talking to herself, not to him, as she tries to define as honestly as she can what she can look forward to. This honesty is moving because it comes at the cost of keeping her hopes alive. Her "mind" and "body" are equal to the darkness that they know is her destiny, but her heart still needs instruction. She "lingers" in the opening line because part of her would like to postpone her fate, and she will weep at the end of her journey because the loss she knows is coming will be too much to bear silently. But in showing such feeling she is not so much weak as simply human, and in going on a journey she knows will end in disappointment she is being true to the role of lover, a role that finally seems more important than blaming the man who leaves her or indulging in her sorrow. Her resignation, it's true, does not keep her from mocking the claims of the "you" to be a real lover ("[You] wanted to meet me, not bring me home"), but the language is studiedly simple, even homely, as an indirect rebuke to the lover's artfulness:

> Oh, if you knew what you do not know
> I could be in the world remembering this.

In not harping on his ignorance, merely asserting it as a fact that has kept her from leaving "this" darkness for the "world," she impresses the reader with the settled conviction of her insight. Through her restraint she attains by the end of the poem the kind of dignity that the myth itself does not give to Eurydice, who tends in traditional versions to be a passive object of love rather than an active agent in her own right. If the man of this poem entails a revision of the myth by falling below the model, the woman revises the myth by rising above it, by acting out the demands of her love despite her clear knowledge that it will never be reciprocated.

In first-person poems like "Sirens" and "Eurydice" that offer a revision of a traditional myth, the poet is present not only immediately, as a participant in the plot of the poem, but also indirectly, as a critic of the tradition that she is borrowing. When the revision is radical, the poet may sometimes find it useful to drop the first person for the impersonal third person to establish a voice that is detached and objective. Such a poem tends to incorporate enough of the myth in the retelling so that it sounds not so much like a rejection of the premises of the story but like a fresh slant on traditional materials. Here is Stephen Dobyns's poem "Long Story":

There must have been a moment after the expulsion
from the Garden when the animals were considering
what to do next and just who was in charge.
The bear flexed his muscles, the tiger flashed
his claws, and even the porcupine thought himself
fit to rule and showed off the knife points
of his quills. No one noticed the hairless creatures,
with neither sharp teeth, nor talons, they were too puny.
It was then Cain turned and slew his own brother
and Abel's white body lay sprawled in the black dirt
as if it had already lain cast down forever.
What followed was an instant of prophetic thought
as the trees resettled themselves, the grass
dug itself deeper into the ground and all
grew impressed by the hugeness of Cain's desire.
He must really want to be boss, said the cat.
This was the moment when the animals surrendered
the power of speech as they crept home to the bosoms
of their families, the prickly ones, the smelly ones,
the ones they hoped would never do them harm.
Who could envy Cain his hunger? Better to be circumspect
and silent. Better not to want the world too much.

Left alone with the body of his brother, Cain began
to assemble the words about what Abel had done
and what he had been forced to do in return.
It was a long story. It took his entire life
to tell it. And even then it wasn't finished.
How great language had to become to encompass
its deft evasions and sly contradictions,
its preenings and self-satisfied gloatings.
Each generation makes a contribution, hoping
to have got it right at last. The sun rises
and sets. The leaves flutter like a million
frightened hands. Confidently, we step forward
and tack a few meager phrases onto the end.[8]

Much of the power of this retelling comes from its willingness to accept a great deal of the myth it revises, so that it seems to be offered
more as a friendly addition than as a reevaluation of the Biblical perspective. Here is no Gnostic recasting of the Fall that presents God as
a tyrant and the serpent as an agent of a higher order. The poet accepts the traditional Biblical message about man's sinfulness, and the
added scene only intensifies our sense of that sinfulness by raising the
question whether fallen man has lost his original claim to rule over
nature. Man does regain his dominance in the course of the poem,
but not by the superior strength of his reason, not from being closer
to God than to the animals, but from being more bestial, more ruth-
less in asserting a blind will to power. And the animals, frightened
and disgusted by an appetite in man that is boundless, retreat into
silence. Man alone is left with the power of speech, which turns out
not to be a sign of his godlike intelligence but merely the practical
instrument by which he can rationalize his grasping. The traditional
story of the Fall, criticized most commonly today as a libel against
human nature, turns out, in this bitter, Swiftian revision, to be some-

thing of a whitewash. The history of human culture is the history of man's pathetic attempts to divert attention from his moral ugliness. While nature trembles in fear, man "confidently" adds what he believes to be the clinching self-justifying argument, though against the million frightened leaves the "few brave sentences" seem pitifully inadequate.

In a dark poem like "Long Story," written from the impersonal point of view, the problem of self-inflation does not arise in any obvious way from the use of myth, not only because its point of view is impersonal but also because the myth is used to humble man rather than to exalt him. In fact the use of myth here seems to be an act of aesthetic modesty, a counterpoise to the claims to authority implicit in this general attack on human nature. If the poet had spoken directly, without the mediation of myth, his indignation would have risked sounding posturing and presumptuous. In using the myth here he presents himself not as a would-be Jeremiah but only as a reteller of comic beast fables, a homely Aesop. The pose is so successful, supported as it is by prosy rhythms and comic details, that we accept the poem's ambitious amending of one of the founding myths of our culture.

Dobyns's third-person mode of retelling the story of the Fall offers a kind of speculative distance not allowed to first-person poems in which the speaker sees a strand of his life as analogous to an episode in an archetypal plot. Here is a speaker who can stand back and speculate quietly about the origins of human power rather than one trying to understand through myth his private condition. But one can also make just as general and far-reaching an evaluation through the first person if the speaker is not the poet but a character from the myth itself. This kind of dramatic monologue has a long history behind it, and was already an established genre by the time of Ovid's *Heroides*. When used conservatively it may be offered simply as a speech that a mythic figure might have been likely to make at an important moment in the traditional story, or in the case of Tennyson's *Ulysses,* which treats Ulysses in old age, what he might be likely to say in circumstances not covered by the story. It's easy to go wrong in such a poem, easy to make the revision sound like the poet's total substitution rather than the revelation of possibility latent in the story itself; but when successful the directness of the presentation carries a particular power. For my example here I want to use a poem from Louise Glück's *The Wild Iris.* In most of the poems in the book the speaker and her husband are presented as contemporary versions of Eve and Adam in a fallen Eden, with the poet unable to make contact with any divine presence and only fitfully listening to the advice she receives from the natural inhabitants of her garden. But in a few poems the god of Genesis speaks directly to the poet in particular and to mankind in general. "Retreating Wind" is a good example of the genre:

> When I made you, I loved you.
> Now I pity you.
>
> I gave you all you needed:
> bed of earth, blanket of blue air—
>
> As I get further away from you
> I see you more clearly.
> Your souls should have been immense by now,
> not what they are,
> small talking things—
>
> I gave you every gift,
> blue of the spring morning,
> time you didn't know how to use—
> you wanted more, the one gift
> reserved for another creation.

Whatever you hoped,
you will not find yourselves in the garden,
among growing plants.
Your lives are not circular like theirs:

your lives are bird's flight
which begins and ends in stillness—
which *begins* and *ends,* in form echoing
this arc from the white birch
to the apple tree.[9]

As in the original retelling of the Fall, most of the blame is placed on human shoulders. But now the wish to taste the tree of knowledge is seen not as simple disobedience to God's command but as a kind of moral stupidity that prevents us from understanding the particular gifts this particular creation has to offer, a blunder that cuts us off from the possibility of a spiritual growth far greater than that allowed by any grasping at knowledge. Our hunger for knowledge has only left us "small talking things," but we might have been unimaginably "immense." How does the poet get away with allowing God to speak directly to her and to the world, with a voice that is meant to be serious, not parodic? Part of the reason we grant the pronouncement authority has to do with the tone of this divine speaker, calm, not angry, disappointed but not disgusted, critical but not querulous, a tone that is supported by the short, almost staccato phrases that seem right for an absent god, driven to speech by the complaints of the poet, as opposed to an oratorical god who enjoys laying down the law. And as we might expect of a remote god, his explanations, however simple the language he uses, however homely the natural images, are not fully comprehensible to our human understanding. What does he mean by telling us our souls could have grown immense without the knowledge of good and evil that comes with tasting the forbidden fruit? How could such a spiritual enlargement be brought to pass merely by our being at one with nature, with feeling the earth our "bed" and the sky our "blanket," in harmony with the cyclical process of the seasons? We are convinced that the speaker has genuine grounds for his disappointment, but we can't be sure exactly what those grounds are. The poet's power to imagine such a response to her own complaints gives those complaints indirect support. It establishes for the speaker's *ethos* the virtue of discrimination, her ability to imagine positions that would effectively undermine her own. But as the recipient of God's reprimand, rather than its composer, the poet also enacts the virtue of humility. She, like the rest of the race, has disappointed God by her deeds and lacks the wisdom to understand exactly the deepest source of her failure. Pride gives her the power to imagine God addressing her, and humility allows her to imagine the address not fully clear to her. This failure of communication is touchingly rendered at the end by the image God chooses in contrasting the circles of the natural movement to the linear movement of the human. It seems odd that to show man's separation from nature God is imagined using a metaphor that draws an analogy between the human world and the natural, the figure of the bird's flight from "the white birch to the apple tree." Is this another example of the discrepancy the poet imagines between God's explanations and our understanding, or is it a symptom of the poet's need to assert a connection with nature however strong the arguments that prove the connection has been broken forever?

The combination of grand ambition and modesty that Glück's poem embodies is a vivid variation on a similar duality that the other poems we have looked at work to achieve in their use of myth; for they all make great claims for the importance of their subjects, and all work to qualify those claims by a modesty that recognizes certain limitations in their speakers' positions. In the Romantic poems of Yeats and Gilbert the speakers are convinced that the women they have loved belong to a high, heroic order, but they also know that they have paid a price for their privileged role of witness. And the women who speak the poems of Gerstler and Gregg, though inhabiting their myths more fully in some respects than the men, find that the myths themselves are problematic. Gerstler's speaker is frustrated by the limited role that her lover assigns her, and Gregg's speaker is matched with a man who can't make the kind of commitment to the ideal model that she achieves. The myth in all cases enlarges the scope of the lovers' problems, giving them a kind of immortal status, releasing them from the world of common prose; but the grander perspective also allows the speakers to understand more fully and sharply the restrictions placed on their freedom. And Dobyns's speaker, in the act of offering a bold emendation of one of the most basic myths of our culture, deposes man from his place in the moral chain of being, placing him beneath the animals, not above them.

The modesty of these ambitious poems is underscored by their sense of audience. These are poems that make great claims, but all but Glück's speaker seem private, their speakers talking more to themselves than to a public audience. In Yeats's poem, the speaker tells of spending his whole life trying to make the world appreciate his lady as much he does, but the account of this effort is not directed to "the coming time" but narrated as part of a private act of self-understanding, as an attempt to define how he feels about his life when he looks back on it from his personal perspective. And Gilbert's speaker, though he ends with a grand statement about the superiority of essence to mode, presents this statement not to convince the world but to formulate for himself the importance of his recollections, to assure himself he has understood his wife's essence though cut off from her presence. The problem of address is complicated somewhat in the poems of Gerstler and Gregg, in which women address a "you" directly. But in both cases the "you" seems unreachable. Gerstler's speaker may still be trying to chide the man into action, but she seems resigned to the fact that he will never escape his perspective; and Gregg's speaker addresses a "you" whose attention she has no hope of winning, even for a moment. In Dobyns's impersonal, third-person poem, one can imagine the speaker addressing the reader directly, but the casual opening suggests more a private meditation than a public argument. "There must have been a moment after the expulsion" is a speculation about probabilities rather than an announcement of a new gospel. At the end of the poem the speaker does make categorical statements about the origins of language and culture, statements that seem addressed to all of us as the sons and daughters of fallen Adam. But these very assertions are so focused on mocking our confidence in language, in pointing out its corruption in self-serving lies, that they throw the issue of address into question. In Glück's poem, the only one that might be called fully public, the speech of God can be regarded as free of moral contamination that Dobyns's speaker imagines inherent in human language, but it serves mainly to remind us that God's ways are not finally our ways. In giving God a voice at the moment she suggests that human reasons and divine reasons are not commensurate, Glück's dramatic monologue expresses still another mode of the weaving of ambition and humility that gives a particular drama to the best mythic poems.

CHAPTER SEVEN

Poetry as Liberation

THE PREMISE OF THIS BOOK, that to be convincing writers must create in their poems speakers that exhibit certain virtues, implies that the modesty or ambition discussed in the last chapter, like the passion, discrimination, and inclusiveness discussed in the first, are aspects of rhetorical strategy, just as in political debate the character that the debater chooses to project is a calculated part of the argument. In both cases the possibility exists that the virtues claimed are not actually possessed. But a timid or lazy writer who praises courage or industry is not necessarily a hypocrite, as the debater may be said to be, because we recognize that the speaker of a poem is a fabrication, related only indirectly to the person who sits down to write, and more likely to express an admired, imagined self than an empirical or historical one.

To say that a persuasive speaker must embody certain virtues does not of course mean that the most effective speakers are those that present themselves as flawless. Just as we noted, at the beginning of the first chapter, that no one is likely to listen to a speaker too confident of his knowledge, so no one will listen to one who seems too virtuous, too good to be true; and few will like a speaker they manage to believe if he claims a moral position far above that of ordinary life. Poets whose speakers confess moral failures are usually on safer ground than those celebrating their moral triumphs. But even a confession, if it is aesthetically effective, will imply certain virtues: the honesty and humility, say, that confronts inadequacies directly, and the ambition implied by judging oneself by the highest standards. Above all, convincing speakers, whether proud or modest, aloof or familiar, will make us believe that they are free. In terms of the three virtues I began with, they will show themselves free to express what they feel without constraint, free in their being able to evaluate their attitudes and actions without self-deception, prejudice, and defensiveness, and free in their comprehending without insularity the largest implications of their positions. In this final chapter I want to explore the nature of this freedom more fully, using as my inspiration Emerson's bold assertion in his essay "The Poet" that "poets are liberating gods":

We are symbols, and inhabit symbols; workmen, work, and tools, words and things, birth and death, all are emblems; but we sympathize with the symbols, and, being infatuated with the economical uses of things, we do not know that they are thoughts. The poet, by an ulterior intellectual perception, gives them a power which makes their old use forgotten, and puts eyes and a tongue into every dumb and inanimate object. . . . He knows why the plain or meadow of space was strown with these flowers we call suns and moons and stars; why the great deep is adorned with animals, with men, and gods; for in every word he speaks he rides on them as the horses of thought. [. . .]

If the imagination intoxicates the poet, it is not inactive in other men. The metamorphosis excites in the beholder an emotion of joy. The use of symbols has a certain power of emancipation and exhilaration for all men. We seem to be touched by a wand which makes us dance and run about happily, like children. We are like persons who come out of a cave or cellar into the open air. This is the effect

on us of tropes, fables, oracles and all poetic forms. Poets are thus
liberating gods. Men have really got a new sense, and found within
their world, another world, or nest of worlds; for, the metamorphosis once seen, we divine that it does not stop.[1]

Here, Emerson grounds his belief in the liberating power of poetry
on the figurative nature of poetic language. By drawing an analogy
between nature and mind, poetic metaphor converts natural facts into
vehicles for thought. The world that is regarded by the practical intelligence as the nonhuman reality which limits human possibility is
revealed by the imagination to be a means toward self-expression
and self-understanding. To accept this proposition we need not accept Emerson's idealist metaphysics, his faith that the world has been
created by spirit for the specific purpose of revealing to our particular
conscious minds unconscious and universal truth. All that is required
is an acceptance of the belief that metaphoric poems ask to be read as
if the analogies were true. This request is one that the skeptical critics
treated in the introduction are not likely to grant. For them, an attempt to ground the poet's thought in nature can be read as an attempt, deliberate or unwitting, to evade the fact that the insights of
the poet are mediated by the conventions of his culture, that his figures are merely projections of his own prejudices on a world he never
confronts directly. Emerson would likely answer such a charge by arguing that it may describe metaphors that fail to convince but not
those that do. To use the distinction he borrowed from Coleridge, we
can say, on his behalf, that an effective metaphor will seem to be the
product not of the fancy but of the imagination, presenting not an
arbitrary association in the mind of the poet but the discovery of the
way in which matter and spirit are actually linked together. Whether
or not the linkage is true in fact to the nature of reality, the reader
will be moved, Emerson might argue, *as if* it were true, and this sub-
junctive belief is enough for both speaker and reader to be suddenly

exalted by a sense of power. For a moment the impervious and ob-structing world appears to be conformable to human thought and feeling.

For Emerson the liberating effects of poetry are most dramatic in poems of bardic inspiration, in which bold figures are used to repu-diate any submission to the facts of the world; but even a poem with-out any figurative language may be liberating in his terms because it presents us with a physical world organized to reveal human mean-ing. So for my example of a poem that fits Emerson's expectations of liberation, I want to look at Robert Frost's "Mending Wall," which is quiet in voice and almost wholly lacking in metaphors.

> Something there is that doesn't love a wall,
> That sends the frozen-ground-swell under it,
> And spills the upper boulders in the sun;
> And makes gaps even two can pass abreast.
> The work of hunters is another thing:
> I have come after them and made repair
> Where they have left not one stone on a stone,
> But they would have the rabbit out of hiding,
> To please the yelping dogs. The gaps I mean,
> No one has seen them made or heard them made,
> But at spring mending-time we find them there.
> I let my neighbor know beyond the hill;
> And on a day we meet to walk the line
> And set the wall between us once again.
> We keep the wall between us as we go.
> To each the boulders that have fallen to each.
> And some are loaves and some so nearly balls
> We have to use a spell to make them balance:
> 'Stay where you are until our backs are turned!'
> We wear our fingers rough with handling them.

Oh, just another kind of outdoor game,
One on a side. It comes to little more:
There where it is we do not need the wall:
He is all pine and I am apple orchard.
My apple trees will never get across
And eat the cones under his pines, I tell him.
He only says, 'Good fences make good neighbors.'
Spring is the mischief in me, and I wonder
If I could put a notion in his head:
'*Why* do they make good neighbors? Isn't it
Where there are cows? But here there are no cows.
Before I built a wall I'd ask to know
What I was walling in or walling out,
And to whom I was like to give offense.
Something there is that doesn't love a wall,
That wants it down.' I could say 'Elves' to him,
But it's not elves exactly, and I'd rather
He said it for himself. I see him there
Bringing a stone grasped firmly by the top
In each hand, like an old-stone savage armed.
He moves in darkness as it seems to me,
Not of woods only and the shade of trees.
He will not go behind his father's saying,
And he likes having thought of it so well
He says again, 'Good fences make good neighbors.'[2]

The poem overtly raises the issue of freedom in that it is based on the contrast between the poet who is able to stand back and criticize the limits of proverbial wisdom and the neighbor who "will not go behind his father's saying." What Emerson might especially appreciate here is the way the theme is embodied through the ordinary occasion of having to repair a wall, the way it gives to the practical chore moral and political implications. To say that "something there is that doesn't love a wall" is to read the natural forces working to topple the stones as an analogue for psychic forces that resist protective barriers between people, pushing toward a deeper connection. Outward facts are being used to body forth inner ones, and the effect is empowering because it suggests a poet who makes the world express his deepest concerns. This power is underscored by the reversal of traditional expectation that the reading entails. The repair of the wall that might conventionally be regarded as repair of the social fabric is presented here as an obstacle to turning "good neighbors" into good friends. The man who believes he is a force for civil harmony turns out to be, in the poet's only, but telling, metaphor, "an old-stone savage armed," an enemy to a deeper kind of union that he lacks the imagination to appreciate. And the poet who would rather play than work becomes through play the spokesman for a higher kind of building. The state of culture, the poem seems to imply, turns out to be all too close to what Hobbes might call the state of nature, and the state of nature an image of a truer human relation than the one that current cultural habit can provide.

While the giving of a symbolic meaning to a commonplace setting might be for Emerson the most important stylistic device for enacting a liberating perspective, the plot and pacing of the poem are relevant in this regard as well. The speaker develops his theme leisurely. His opening remarks about the seasonal forces toppling the wall do not seem to be more than casual observation, and the poem is more than half over before we realize that the poet and the neighbor differ in their attitudes to the work of repair. The leisurely development gives formal support to the poet's questioning the value of the practical enterprise. Free of the compulsion to rebuild the wall, the poet can calmly reflect on alternatives, moving around his subject without pressing toward argument and conclusion. This freedom is perhaps most obvious in the five-line aside (lines 5 to 10) about the gaps in the fence that are not the subject of the poem at hand, the gaps left by hunters. This clarification is not really required, for we are told in line 2 that the "frost heaves" cause the kind of gaps the poet wants to talk about; but it does serve to make an argument about the character of the speaker. As a casual interpolation, it suggests the speaker's freedom from the kind of univocal plot that the laconic neighbor seems gripped by. The neighbor has only one thing on his mind, but the poet has many things, and if the neighbor isn't interested then the reader may be. In any case the poet won't exclude an interesting detour for the sake of neatness. This leisureliness is also suggested by the repetition of the first line of the poem at line 20. The poet seems to have moved slowly in a wide arc and returned with more experience to give the line a deeper meaning. But when the neighbor repeats his one line about good neighbors, he is only revealing his rigidity, his being stuck fast in a single track. In associating narrative leisure with freedom, the poem does in small and comic terms what Melville's *Moby Dick* does on an epic scale in giving its narrator the ability to digress from a clear moral meaning. Every time Ishmael stops his story of the search for the whale to luxuriate in the lore of the whale, he declares his independence from the kind of compulsion that drives Ahab to ask only one question of all he meets, "Hast seen the White Whale?" Digression means openness to many questions; aggression means bondage to a single way of looking at the world.

For Emerson, the great enemy of the liberating perspective of poetry is the perspective of history, at least of history as he sees it as traditionally practiced, where the writer emphasizes the weight of the past on the present and suggests that we are the product of forces outside our will rather than the shapers of our own individual destinies. He would have seen the current skeptical formulation of this doctrine, its doubt about the ability of anyone to escape the dominant discourse of the time, as only a more radical and more explicit version of these assumptions, and would probably have dealt with it by ac-

cepting it in a limited and less absolute way, developing the concession he makes in "The American Scholar":

> As no air-pump can by any means make a perfect vacuum, so
> neither can any artist entirely exclude the confessional, the local, the
> perishable from his book, or write a book of pure thought, that shall
> be as efficient, in all respects, to a remote posterity, as to contem-
> poraries, or rather to the second age.

But in the context of his essay this acknowledgment is used not to
instill modesty in writers but to encourage them to throw off submis-
siveness to the monuments of the past, which, however grand, cannot, because of some tincture of the "local," be fully relevant to the
present. "Each age," the passage continues, "must write its own
books; or rather, each generation for the next succeeding. The books
of an older generation will not fit this." In "The American Scholar,"
the same message is directed to the would-be historian. Scholarship is
valuable, Emerson argues, to the extent that the scholar is able to
overcome his diffidence before the past and use historical facts the
same way he is encouraged to use the facts of nature, as instruments
for the articulating of his own discoveries. In his essay "History," Emerson defines this notion of useful history as a form of projected au-
tobiography: "The student is to read history actively and not passively; to esteem his own life the text, and books the commentary.
Thus compelled, the Muse of history will utter oracles, as never to
those who do not respect themselves." The more deeply we explore
ourselves, the assumption seems to be here, the more confident we
can be that we are discovering what is most universal about mankind.
As he expresses it in a passage of "Self-Reliance" already referred to
in the introduction, "To believe that what is true for you in your private heart is true for all men—that is genius."

Today's reader may have trouble sharing Emerson's faith in the
ability of the individual to contain the experience of the world, and

may shake his head in disbelief as Emerson proclaims again in "History": "To the poet, to the philosopher, to the saint, all things are friendly and sacred, all events profitable, all days holy, all men divine." But the contrast drawn here between the authority of the poet and that of the traditional historian is kin to the distinction Aristotle makes in the *Poetics* when he calls poetry more philosophical than history. History, as he says in his famous formulation, is concerned with what has happened and poetry with what might happen or could happen. Poets, unlike historians, claim to know what is universal about human behavior, and such a claim is still made today even in first-person poems that insist on the particularity and subjectivity of their occasions. What is true for me, the poet claims, is true for everyone, so that the most intimate love poem possesses a truth about love in general, and the most personal elegy throws light on the meaning of all loss. Thus in Frost's poem the speaker and the neighbor, though defined as individuals, are also types, so that their conflict, however mundane its embodiment, has a universal significance. And even a poem whose speaker is far more modest than Frost's cannot avoid the claim to typicality, as any poet learns who tries to make use in a poem of a journal entry and discovers that it cannot sustain the expectation of general reference placed on it by the genre.

The liberating claim that the particulars of poetry have universal significance is supported in the *Poetics* by Aristotle's claim that plot, the central element of drama, is a function of character as well as situation. The central characters of epic and tragedy are not in full control of their own lives, but these genres focus attention on the moments when its protagonists make significant choices or judgments. To use an example familiar to Aristotle, the *Iliad,* unlike a history of the Trojan War, omits many of the most famous incidents of the war to focus on a single episode in the tenth year, beginning with Achilles' angry removal from battle, progressing to his angry reentry, and concluding with his final calm. Achilles' choices are sharply restricted. He can choose a life of honor only by choosing an early death, and his nobility is partly a function of his understanding how beleaguered he is by forces he cannot alter. But the poem constructs its massive account of the war around the hero's limited choice, to fight or not to fight, and to this extent the action of the poem is typical not only in its account of the causes of war but also in its affirmation of individual freedom.

The importance of this affirmation for Aristotle is bound up with certain facts about the nature of the reader's (or listener's) emotional engagement. To be moved by a fiction we must be willing to identify on some level with its protagonist, and we find it hard to identify with someone who has no significant control over his own life. And what is true for Aristotle about the protagonist of a play can be applied as well to the speaker of a poem. The speaker may win our interest in the victims he observes in the world around him, but the minute he presents himself as a victim the reader withdraws. Even if we are convinced that the poet is justified in his lament, and not merely trying to evade responsibility, we feel reluctant to let ourselves become involved in the problems of someone who has played no part in his own misfortune, who has been allowed no significant choices.

In poetry that is not narrative, where the action takes the form of a sequence of thoughts, not a sequence of deeds, the assertion of freedom is found most basically in the poet's ability to give his situation significance, to impose his own meaning on it rather than let others define it for him. This pattern is overt in "Mending Wall," as the speaker rejects the neighbor's view of wall-mending in favor of his own. How easy it would be to ruin this poem by making the speaker see himself as a victim, a man starved for friendship in a world of Philistines, forced to build a wall he sees no need for in order to placate a society that thrives on division. But Frost's poet remains always at ease and in control. He is the one who notices the gaps and informs his neighbor, as if willing for the neighbor's peace of mind to participate in an action he sees no need for. And he almost seems successful in getting the neighbor to play at casting spells on the stones so they can stay where they're supposed to. Finally he decides out of quiet pride not to lecture his neighbor when the man is unable to rise to the occasion. And throughout he emphasizes his own control by keeping the poem fixed in the present, where choice is still meaningful for him and his neighbor, rather than presenting it as a history no longer accessible to revision. If the poem may be said to have any limitation with regard to freedom, it results not from the poet's denial of freedom to himself but from his denying it to the neighbor in the concluding metaphor of the stone savage. Though the comparison is vivid, its implications seem unnecessarily restrictive, reading the neighbor's commitment to the wall as mere provincial prejudice. Why, we wonder, could Frost not have given the neighbor a serious worldview that regards symbolic boundaries as necessary? Why couldn't he have made his poem about the conflict between two views of human possibility rather than between imagination and ignorance?

In most successful poems about ignorance, the benighted figure is not someone opposed to the poet but an aspect of the poet's own nature. The speaker is ambivalent, facing a problem that invites opposing interpretations and resolutions. For such a poem to be effective, we have to feel that the speaker's difficulties are not being used to excuse him from taking a stand but to suggest a need to confront a divided commitment within himself. For my example here, I want to use a poem by a contemporary of Emerson's, Frederick Goddard Tuckerman, a writer of sonnets who manages to exhibit very little of the bardic confidence Emerson enjoins, writing poems that tend instead to dwell on the poet's uncertainties:

> That boy, the farmer said, with hazel wand
> Pointing him out, half by the haycock hid,
> Though bare sixteen, can work at what he's bid

From sun till set, to cradle, reap, or band.
I heard the words, but scarce could understand
Whether they claimed a smile or gave me pain:
Or was it aught to me, in that green lane,
That all day yesterday, the briars amid,
He held the plough against the jarring land
Steady, or kept his place among the mowers
Whilst other fingers, sweeping for the flowers,
Brought from the forest back a crimson stain?
Was it a thorn that touched the flesh, or did
The pokeberry spit purple on my hand?[3]

Listening to a farmer praise a sixteen-year-old boy for his skill and stamina in the work of plowing and harvesting, the poet does not know whether to share the farmer's admiration or to be pained by the boy's being deprived of the pleasures of boyhood. The poet himself, we learn in the central lines of the poem, has spent his day not working but gathering flowers. Now he wonders if the boy's work can be read as a critical commentary on what may seem like his own self-indulgent idleness. The use of "other fingers" to refer to his own actions suggests in its indirection some embarrassment. Whereas in the Frost poem the neighbor represents a false view of civility that the poet repudiates, the farmer here expresses a view the speaker can respect, based on the notion of the world as fallen, a place of conflict in which we are commanded to win our living from the earth with the sweat of our brows. Against this perspective the poet indirectly opposes the notion of nature as a source of spiritual companionship. But the poet can appreciate simultaneously the truth of both views and so is in a quandary as to how to evaluate his own experience, a quandary that is expressed symbolically by the concluding question. The crimson stain on the poet's hand after a day of flower gathering can be interpreted in two ways. If the stain is the poet's own blood,

drawn by a scratch of a briar, it may have the traditional meaning
of the stain of sin and mortality, and therefore may reinforce the
farmer's Biblical view of the human condition. If the stain is the juice
of the pokeberry, then it would seem nature's mark of friendly recognition at a brotherly presence. But while the poem gives us a poet
who is stymied by this question, uncertain about the meaning of his
own life, it also suggests indirectly the poet's power to define precisely
what his options are. The speaker is able to find in the homeliest of
facts the largest of implications, true to Emerson's aesthetic of the liberating symbol. And the particular implications he finds suggest that
he is not the product of one culturally dominant code but is able to
inhabit two opposed interpretive systems simultaneously. He can
view his world both as a Puritan would view it and as a Romantic. His
choice may be difficult but his very ability to define and focus it suggests that he has the distance required to make it meaningful.

If poems about ignorance involve a liberating clarification, what
about poems where freedom is threatened more directly, not by a lack
of knowledge but a lack of power? Don't the vast majority of poems
fall into this category, whether the poet faces the sickness of the social
order that he can't cure or some private loss that he can't prevent?
Such a poem, I want to argue, succeeds to the extent that the poet is
able both to recognize this constriction of choice and to resist it in
some significant way by the power of his or her own articulations. In
a public poem like Lowell's "For the Union Dead," this effort, as we
saw in chapter 5, means that the poet confronts the wrong presented
with the appropriate feelings of anger or contempt rather than with a
passive shrug. In private poems it means doing justice to the loss by
trying to wrest from it some affirmation of value, if only the value of
loving what has proven too weak to prevail against the forces ranged
against it. So Dickinson's quiet speaker in "The Heart Asks Pleasure
First" counters, as we saw in chapter 2, the increasing constriction of
life with her power of distilled generalization, achieving a dignity that

her list of narrowing possibilities cannot undermine, a dignity that is enhanced by the naming of her "Inquisitor" at the end of the poem, which adds a cool scorn to the tone of calm acceptance, scorn for whoever is responsible for the heartless dispensation that has been granted us.

Poets like Lowell and Dickinson assert the poet's power to weigh the world and find it wanting, and this power leads to a genre of poem that sets itself even more deliberately against history, the poem that openly opposes the world as given to the world that the poet would like to have. For the historian concerned with why things have happened as they have, the world as found tends to comprise the real world, while to poets, concerned, as Aristotle says, with what should be as much as with what is, the world as found is only one of many possibilities. Beside any path actually taken from one point in time to another runs a myriad of ghostly paths of the might-have-been, all at one time equally possible; and this perspective means that poetry often has to find an important place for regret, for the exploring of lost possibility, as well as for the accepting of the realities of the moment. This different attitude toward possibility is even more obvious with regard to the future. To the extent that historians are interested in writing about the future at all, they tend to concentrate on predictions based on extrapolating from those forces they have identified as salient in the past. But for the poet, the future tends to be an alternative to the past, not an extension of it, the home of unembodied possibilities that need to be kept alive in order to give purpose and value to the present. Poetry, in other words, makes a significant place for wishing, in public forms as well as private, though the love poem has probably been the genre most indebted to wishing for some of its most ambitious examples. So the speaker of Marvell's "To His Coy Mistress" wishes not merely to possess his lady but to live in a world rich enough in space and time to allow him to court her with all the leisure and lavishness that she deserves. Circumstances may force Marvell's lovers to compromise, but the recognition of how much is lost in that compromise is just as important as the recognition of what is salvaged. And many poems fulfill themselves simply in expressing wishes that have no chance at all of ever being embodied.

The poets of the Romantic period tended to be particularly sympathetic to impractical wishes, identifying our enthusiasms and longings with our deepest humanity, so I will end my discussion of poetry as liberation by examining two poems squarely in that tradition. First, Blake's famous love poem "Ah Sun-flower," which contains a double wish, to leave the world and to transform it:

> Ah Sun-flower! weary of time,
> Who countest the steps of the Sun,
> Seeking after that sweet golden clime
> Where the traveller's journey is done:
>
> Where the Youth pined away with desire,
> And the pale Virgin shrouded in snow,
> Arise from their graves and aspire,
> Where my Sun-flower wishes to go.[4]

In wishing to enter the golden clime of the sun, the sunflower, rooted as it is in the earth, might seem to be indulging in a wish as fruitless as the wish of the coy mistress in Marvell's poem; but here, as the opening "ah" suggests, the speaker seems to sympathize without practical reservations. The very name "sun-flower," and the physical resemblance behind the name, suggests that the poet reads the longing less as a refusal to confront the harsh facts of mortality than as an expression of the sunflower's deepest nature. To be a sunflower, we must presume, means to long to emulate the sun. And to feel a kinship with the sunflower as the poet does—it is *my* sunflower in the last line— is to acknowledge a similar longing for a "sweet golden clime" that can't be found on earth. This longing gets defined in the second stanza in terms of sexual love. The pining lover and the snowy virgin long for a love that is reciprocated and expressed without reserve, for a kind of complete love that, while thwarted in the world of time, can embody itself unimpeded in the world beyond time. And the speaker seems to accept their longing as a sign of spiritual ambition, not of naiveté. But the speaker may also be suggesting here that the lovers may have more ways to resist the world than by wishing to leave it. For we have no clear evidence that the poet hankers like the sunflower and the lovers for the realm "where the traveller's journey is done." The question of the poet's position arises in part because it's not clear in what way time is to blame for thwarting the pining lover and the snowy virgin. Isn't their problem less a matter of a mortality and fragility that restrict their external freedom than it is a matter of internal, self-imposed inhibitions? Could these lovers have internalized to some extent the values of their times that inhibit sexual expression? Unwilling to abandon completely their hopes of sexual fulfillment, they end by reserving them for another world, whereas a deeper kind of insight might allow them to see this world as the proper field for love. That their hopes in the golden world may be misplaced is suggested by the poem's circular syntax, which introduces the pining lovers in the second stanza in a way that leads us to expect not longing but fulfillment, by a "where" that we assume refers to the place "where the traveller's journey is done." The confusion seems to suggest that longing for happiness is endless as long as happiness is seen as something external to the self. If the lovers are going to reach fulfillment, they will have to give up the wish for a supernal realm and reach a deeper kind of vision that allows them to turn their wishes toward embracing the hidden possibilities of the moment. In this reading the "ah" of the opening suggests the speaker's pity as well as empathy, pity for the creatures full of spiritual longing whose imaginations are insufficiently free. They hunger for beauty but don't yet know where to look for it. In wishing to escape the world of time they may endow time with too much power.

The point of view that I ascribe to Blake's poet here bears a strong kinship to the perspective of Whitman's speaker in a poem like "Song of Myself," though Whitman's "Walt" is even more emphatic than Blake's speaker in setting wishing aside for a heightened seeing. For him, all possibility is available to anyone who is able to enter the present with a free mind, open to the wonders of empathy with the world at hand. To wish is to accuse the moment of being somehow inadequate to human need, whereas the poet-prophet has come to tell us that the moment we have, seen rightly, is infinitely satisfying. For an example of a true wish poem among American Romantics, we need to turn to someone with a stronger sense of human limitation. Though there are many candidates to choose from, Poe being perhaps the most obvious, it seems appropriate to close this discussion of freedom by turning to Dickinson, since she and Whitman have been contrasted throughout. Here is her ardent love poem "Wild Nights—Wild Nights!," in which wishing is given the highest value:

> Wild Nights—Wild Nights!
> Were I with thee
> Wild Nights should be
> Our luxury!
>
> Futile—the Winds—
> To a Heart in port—
> Done with the Compass—
> Done with the Chart!
>
> Rowing in Eden—
> Ah, the Sea!
> Might I but moor—Tonight—
> In Thee![5]

This is a poem of wishing for what is contrary to fact, but it focuses less on frustration than on the joy that would be experienced if the union were possible, devoting itself to an emphatic assertion of the joined lovers' godlike self-sufficiency. It's hard, in fact, to think of a poem where greater claims are made for the value of love, where the joining of lovers creates a realm of such complete safety that it turns a night of violent storm into a luxurious entertainment. Separation thus seems less of a barrier than a tool that allows the poet to affirm the strength of her commitment to her beloved, which remains undiminished. In its confident tone and emphatic rhythms, the poem makes clear that the longing it expresses is not a sign of weakness but a sign of strength, of the lovers' power to create a counterworld that can turn the threats of the ordinary world into pleasures. That the lovers are not weary with life, like Blake's lovers, but are rather enlarging and completing it, is made clear in the last stanza when, having reached the safe harbor of their union, they set out to sea once more. Eden is not a refuge from adventure. It provides its own sea that the lovers take pleasure in exploring together. This paradise is, to be sure, a private one. It contains only two people. But the Biblical name suggests indirectly the bold claim that the power ascribed to the God of Genesis has been transferred to the lovers themselves, who do not merely inhabit the garden, like the original Adam and Eve, but actually bring it into being by the completeness and intensity of their love (or at least would bring it into being were they able to come together). No history book will ever mention this unrealized Eden, no history of public life, or even of private. To find it we have to follow the speaker who has managed to free herself enough from history to visit the Bureau of What Hasn't Happened. She has convinced us that only if we make this visit can the meaning of what in fact has happened be fully revealed.

In resisting history, the speaker of this poem embodies in a radical way the three virtues that we defined in the first chapter as essential

for a convincing speaker. She is passionate in her emphatic assertion of love in defiance of separation, discriminating in her ability to
imagine an alternative state to the one she suffers and to subject that
state to trial, and she shows herself possessed of an inclusive vision
in her associating the personal paradise she imagines for herself and
her beloved with the Eden that everyone is assumed to long for. We
are convinced as we read the poem that we are in the presence of
someone whose company is liberating, someone who takes for her *ars
poetica* an exhortation like the one given to poets at the conclusion
of Auden's "In Memory of W. B. Yeats." She can be said to "Sing
of human unsuccess / In a rapture of distress." While dwelling "in
the prison of [her] days," she teaches "the free" among us "how to
praise."

Notes

Introduction

1. M. H. Abrams develops his classification of critical approaches to art in the first chapter of *The Mirror and the Lamp* (New York: Oxford University Press, 1958). I substitute "world" for the more cosmic term he tends to use for the "not-I," "universe."

2. Yeats numbers himself among "the last romantics" in "Coole Park and Ballylee, 1931," from his book *The Winding Stair and Other Poems,* published in 1933. See his collected *Poems* (New York: Macmillan, 1983), 245.

3. The quotation from Nietzsche is from Walter Kaufman's translation of *The Gay Science* (New York: Random House, 1974), 232.

4. The quotations from Emerson about the need of the poet to turn from the world and the limitations of the "lyrist" are from his essay "The Poet" in volume 3 of the *Complete Works of Ralph Waldo Emerson,* 12 vols. (Boston: Houghton Mifflin, 1903), 41, 9. His definition of "genius" can be found in the essay "Self-Reliance," volume 2, page 45. The entry from his *Journals,* which is dated April 19, 1848, can be found most readily in Bliss Perry's often reprinted *The Heart of Emerson's Journals* (Boston: Houghton Mifflin, 1926), 231. The emphasis in the closing phrase is Emerson's own.

5. The quotation from Richard Ohmann is from his essay "Speech Acts and the Definition of Literature," which appeared in *Philosophy and Rhetoric* 4 (1971): 1–19. Here he uses J. L. Austin's theory of speech acts to develop a

notion of *mimesis* that avoids the problem of proving any direct correspondence between text and world.

6. Charles Altieri expands Ohmann's notion of literature as the imitation of a conventional speech act in his essay "The Poem as Act: A Way to Reconcile Mimetic and Presentational Theories," *Iowa Review* 6 (1975): 103–24. In his important book *Act and Quality* (Amherst: University of Massachusetts Press, 1981), which led me back to these essays, Altieri works out more fully the ways in which speech act theory, supplemented by a reading of Wittgenstein's notions of meaning in action, may be used to describe the way literature engages the world.

7. Wayne Booth's *The Company We Keep: An Ethics of Fiction* was published by the University of California Press in 1988.

ONE. *The Voice of Authority*

1. Jonson's poem, "To the Reader," begins his book *Epigrams* (1616).

2. Yeats's "The Second Coming" was included in his *Michael Robartes and the Dancer* (1921). See the collected *Poems* (New York: Macmillan, 1983), 187.

3. Dickinson's "To fight aloud" is numbered 126 in Thomas Johnson's edition, *The Poems of Emily Dickinson* (Cambridge: Harvard University Press, 1955), and appears on page 90.

4. Williams's "Proletarian Portrait" was included in his book *An Early Martyr* (1935). See volume 1 of *The Collected Poems of William Carlos Williams* (New York: New Directions, 1986), 384.

5. The quotations from Whitman's "Song of Myself" are taken from sections 5 and 15. The sections were not numbered in the first edition (1855).

6. Lowell's "Alfred Corning Clark" was included in *For the Union Dead* (1964) and reprinted in *Selected Poems* (New York: Farrar Straus, 1976), 110–11.

7. O'Hara's "The Day Lady Died" can be found most readily in *Lunch Poems* (San Francisco: City Lights, 1964), 27.

8. Adam Zagajewski's poem "The Generation" can be found in his book *Tremor* (New York: Farrar Straus, 1985), 54–55.

TWO. *Point of View*

1. I use Thomas Johnson's edition, *The Poems of Emily Dickinson* (Cambridge: Harvard University Press, 1955), and follow his numbering for the poems. The poems, not titled, are listed by first lines, with their number in his sequence given in parentheses, followed by the page number: "The Heart Asks Pleasure" (536) 413; "I shall know why—when Time is over" (193) 139; "There's a certain Slant of light" (258) 185; "I'm Nobody! Who are you?" (288) 206; "Some things that fly there be" (89) 72; "The Brain—is wider than the Sky" (632) 486.

2. Williams's poem on the red wheelbarrow first appeared in *Spring and All* (1923), under section XXII. See *The Collected Poems,* page 224.

3. Williams's poem "Self-Portrait" can be found in his *Pictures from Brueghel* (New York: New Directions, 1962), 3.

4. Sylvia Plath's "Last Words" was first published in *Crossing the Water* in 1971. See Ted Hughes, ed., *The Collected Poems of Sylvia Plath* (New York: Harper and Row, 1981), 172.

5. Lisel Mueller's "Things" can be found in her book of new and selected poems, *Alive Together* (Baton Rouge: Louisiana State University Press, 1996), 26.

6. Charles Simic's "Club Midnight" appears in his *Walking the Black Cat* (New York: Harcourt Brace, 1996), 66.

THREE. *Irony*

1. Jack Gilbert's "Games" can be found in his *Monolithos* (New York: Alfred A. Knopf, 1982), 83.

2. Michael Van Walleghen's "Fun at Crystal Lake" can be found in his *More Trouble with the Obvious* (Urbana: University of Illinois Press, 1981), 5–6.

3. Tess Gallagher's "Start Again Somewhere" can be found in her *Under Stars* (Port Townsend: Graywolf Press, 1978), 42–43.

4. The passage from Kierkegaard is from his *The Concept of Irony.* I use the

translation by Howard V. Hong and Edna H. Hong (Princeton: Princeton University Press, 1989), 256–57.

5. Swift's "Description of a City Shower" first appeared in *The Tatler* (1709); it can readily be found in the *Complete Poems* (New York: Penguin, 1983). I quote lines 42–52.

6. The translation of Catullus's "Lugete, O Veneres Cupidinesque" is my own.

7. The quotation from Wayne Booth is from his *A Rhetoric of Irony* (Chicago: University of Chicago Press, 1974). See especially pages 240–77.

8. Allen Ginsberg's "America" appears in *Howl* (San Francisco: City Lights Books, 1956), 31–32.

9. Charles Bernstein's "Emotions of Normal People" appears in his *Dark City* (Los Angeles: Sun and Moon Press, 1994), 89–90.

10. Czeslaw Milosz's "Incantation" can be found in his *Collected Poems* (New York: Ecco Press, 1987), 210.

FOUR. *Political Poetry*

1. Philip Lopate's "Allende" appears in his *The Daily Round* (New York: Sun Press, 1976), 21–22.

2. The quotations from Allen Ginsberg's "Howl" are from *Howl and Other Poems* (San Francisco: City Lights Books, 1959), 9, 17.

3. Robert Lowell's "For Robert Kennedy 1925–1968" can be found in his *Selected Poems* (New York: Farrar, Straus and Giroux, 1976), 176.

4. Sylvia Plath's "Daddy" appears in her *Collected Poems* (New York: Harper and Row, 1981), 222.

5. Tony Hoagland's "My Country" appears in his *Sweet Ruin* (Madison: University of Wisconsin Press, 1992), 9–10.

6. Mark Halliday's poem "Fox Point Health Clinic, 1974" appears in his *Tasker Street* (Amherst: University of Massachusetts Press, 1992), 59–60.

FIVE. *Midcourse Corrections*

1. The quotation from Yeats is from *A Vision* (New York: Macmillan, 1961), 214.

2. Horace's ode on Cleopatra is number 37 in book 1 of the *Odes.* The translation is my own.

3. Lowell's "For the Union Dead" was included in *For the Union Dead* (New York: Farrar Straus, 1964) and can be found in the *Selected Poems* (New York: Farrar Straus, 1976), 135–37.

4. Elizabeth Bishop's "At the Fishhouses" was included in *A Cold Spring* (New York: Farrar Straus, 1955) and can be found in *The Complete Poems* (New York: Farrar Straus, 1983), 64–66.

5. C. K. Williams's poem "From My Window" can be found in his book *Tar* (New York: Random House, 1983), 3–5.

six. *Myth*

1. Yehuda Amichai's "The Place Where I Have Not Been" appears in *Poems,* translated by Assia Gutmann (New York: Harper and Row, 1968), 5.

2. Yeats's "A Woman Homer Sung" was included in *The Green Helmet and Other Poems* (1910) and can be found in *Poems* (New York: Macmillan, 1983), 89–90.

3. Jack Gilbert's "Remembering My Wife" can be found in his *Monolithos* (New York: Alfred A. Knopf, 1982), 48.

4. The passages from Whitman are from section 41 of "Song of Myself," lines 1226–35 in the edition of 1891–92.

5. Dickinson's "One Crucifixion is recorded—only" is numbered 553 in Johnson's edition and appears on page 423.

6. Amy Gerstler's "Sirens" can be found in *Bitter Angel* (San Francisco: North Point Press, 1990), 3.

7. Linda Gregg's "Eurydice" can be found in *Too Bright to See* (Port Townsend: Graywolf Press, 1981), 40.

8. Stephen Dobyns's "Long Story" is included in *Body Traffic* (1990) and can be found in his selected poems, *Velocities* (New York: Viking Penguin, 1994), 249.

9. Louise Glück's "Retreating Wind" appears in *The Wild Iris* (New York: Ecco Press, 1992), 15.

SEVEN. *Poetry as Liberation*

1. The two quotations from Emerson's "The Poet" can be found in the Houghton Mifflin twelve-volume edition (1903), volume 3, the first on pages 20–21 and the second on page 30. The passage from "The American Scholar" can be found in vol. 1, page 88; the passages from "History" in vol. 2, pages 7–8, 10, and 12; and the passage from "Self-Reliance" in vol. 2, page 45.

2. Frost's "Mending Wall" was included in *North of Boston* (1914) and can be found in all subsequent selected editions, including *The Complete Poetry of Robert Frost* (New York: Holt, Rinehart and Winston, 1964), 47.

3. Tuckerman's untitled sonnet, "That boy, the farmer said, with hazel wand," first published in *Sonnets, First Series* in 1860, is included in *The Complete Poems of Frederick Goddard Tuckerman* (New York: Oxford University Press, 1965), 19.

4. Blake's "Ah Sun-flower" was first published in *Songs of Innocence and Experience* in 1794.

5. Dickinson's "Wild Nights—Wild Nights!" is numbered 249 in Johnson's edition and appears on page 179.

Index

The Life of Poetry
POETS ON THEIR ART AND CRAFT

Carl Dennis
Poetry as Persuasion

Michael Ryan
A Difficult Grace: On Poets, Poetry, and Writing

Sherod Santos
A Poetry of Two Minds

Ellen Bryant Voigt
The Flexible Lyric